Facebook® Marketing FOR DUMMIES®

by Paul Dunay and Richard Krueger

WILEY

Wiley Publishing, Inc.

Facebook® Marketing For Dummies®

Published by
Wiley Publishing, Inc.
111 River Street
Hoboken, NJ 07030-5774

www.wiley.com

Copyright © 2010 by Wiley Publishing, Inc., Indianapolis, Indiana

Published by Wiley Publishing, Inc., Indianapolis, Indiana

Published simultaneously in Canada

For general information on our other products and services, please contact our Customer Care Department within the U.S. at 877-762-2974, outside the U.S. at 317-572-3993, or fax 317-572-4002.

For technical support, please visit www.wiley.com/techsupport.

Wiley also publishes its books in a variety of electronic formats. Some content that appears in print may not be available in electronic books.

Library of Congress Control Number: 2009937279

ISBN: 978-0-470-48762-4

Manufactured in the United States of America

10   9   8   7   6   5   4   3

WILEY

About the Authors

Paul Dunay is an award-winning marketer with more than 20 years' success in generating demand and creating buzz for leading technology, consumer products, financial services and professional services organizations.

Paul is Global Managing Director of Services and Social Marketing for Avaya, a global leader in enterprise communications. His unique approach to integrated marketing has led to recognition as a BtoB Magazine Top 25 B2B Marketer of the Year for 2009 and winner of the DemandGen Award for Utilizing Marketing Automation to Fuel Corporate Growth in 2008. He is also a five-time finalist in the Marketing Excellence Awards competition of the Information Technology Services Marketing Association (ITSMA) and a 2005 gold award winner.

Richard Krueger is founder and CEO of About Face Digital, a social media marketing agency specializing in Facebook promotions. Recognized as an online marketing innovator, Mr. Krueger is also co-founder of Samepoint, LLC, a leading social media analytics company. He brings more than 20 years of experience to his roles at both companies.

Mr. Krueger previously served as Chief Marketing Officer for Boonty, Inc., a worldwide digital distributor of casual games. Prior to that, he served as VP of Marketing and Business Development for Kasparov Chess Online, where he led marketing and brand licensing efforts for Garry Kasparov, the former world chess champion. Before his entrepreneurial career, Mr. Krueger worked at several top ten advertising and public relations agencies in New York City. He is a regular blogger and contributes numerous articles to advertising and PR trade journals.

Dedication

We dedicate this book to marketers everywhere who are in the middle of the biggest sea change in marketing history. We believe there has never been a better time to be a marketer, and that tools like Facebook are rewriting the rules. In fact, we believe that Facebook will become the preferred platform for marketers to acquire new customers, interact with existing customers, and sell products and services. We hope that by providing you with straight forward, step-by-step advice, as well as sharing our real-world experiences in marketing companies via Facebook, you'll become better at your craft and thereby take us all to levels in marketing we've yet to explore.

Authors' Acknowledgments

This project could not have succeeded without the help and support of many people who truly helped make this book a success.

First, we would like to acknowledge our families for allowing us to pursue our passion for Facebook Marketing. We appreciate all your understanding and support throughout the time we took away from you to write this book.

We would like to thank the superb team at Wiley. Amy Fandrei, who reached out to us because of our blog and held our hands through the entire process. Susan Cohen, our project editor, who kept us on track every step of the way. James Russell, who helped us conform the book to Dummies standards. And all the other Wiley folks behind the scenes who made the book possible.

Thanks to scores of bloggers, too many to list, who kept us informed about changes at Facebook and what they meant to businesses. Most of all, we'd like to thank Facebook founder Mark Zuckerberg, and his team of young entrepreneurs and software developers, for their vision in realizing the most popular online social network on the planet.

Publisher's Acknowledgments

We're proud of this book; please send us your comments through our online registration form located at http://dummies.custhelp.com. For other comments, please contact our Customer Care Department within the U.S. at 877-762-2974, outside the U.S. at 317-572-3993, or fax 317-572-4002.

Some of the people who helped bring this book to market include the following:

Acquisitions, Editorial, and Media Development

Project Editor: Susan B. Cohen

Acquisitions Editor: Amy Fandrei

Copy Editor: Brian Walls

Technical Editor: Jim Trageser

Editorial Manager: Jodi Jensen

Media Development Project Manager: Laura Moss-Hollister

Media Development Assistant Project Manager: Jenny L. Swisher

Media Development Associate Producer: Shawn Patrick

Editorial Assistant: Amanda Graham

Sr. Editorial Assistant: Cherie Case

Cartoons: Rich Tennant (www.the5thwave.com)

Composition Services

Senior Project Coordinator: Kristi Rees

Layout and Graphics: Ashley Chamberlain, Joyce Haughey, Melissa K. Jester, Christin Swinford, Christine Williams

Proofreaders: Melissa Cossell, Evelyn W. Gibson

Indexer: Beth Palmer

Publishing and Editorial for Technology Dummies

    Richard Swadley, Vice President and Executive Group Publisher

    Andy Cummings, Vice President and Publisher

    Mary Bednarek, Executive Acquisitions Director

    Mary C. Corder, Editorial Director

Publishing for Consumer Dummies

    Diane Graves Steele, Vice President and Publisher

Composition Services

    Debbie Stailey, Director of Composition Services

Contents at a Glance

Table of Contents

Introduction

● ●

*W*ith more than 200 million active users and 250,000 new registrants every day, Facebook has become a virtual world unto itself. But, what started as a dorm room exercise to extend the popular printed college directory of incoming freshmen online, Harvard drop-out Mark Zuckerberg has developed an international organization employing more than 400 programmers, graphic artists, and business development executives (expected to rise to more than 1,000 employees by the end of 2009) with a valuation in excess of $15 billion, depending on who you ask.

For many, Facebook is considered a social experience, a place to reconnect with an old college chum, or "poke" a new friend. But in April 2007, Zuckerberg did something so revolutionary its aftershocks are still felt throughout the business Web. He opened his virtual oasis to allow anyone with a little programming know-how to build applications that take advantage of the platform's *social graph* (that is, network architecture). In that single open software act, Facebook has redefined the rules for marketers looking to gain access to social networks. And it will never be business as usual again.

About This Book

Facebook Marketing For Dummies is the first book to provide you, a marketer, with in-depth analysis into the strategies, tactics, and techniques available to leverage the Facebook community and achieve your business objectives. By breaking down the Web service into its basic features of creating a Facebook Page for your business, adding applications to your Page, hosting an event, creating a Facebook Group, advertising, and buying and selling goods in the Facebook Marketplace, we lay out a user-friendly blueprint to marketing and promoting an organization via Facebook. Furthermore, we cite numerous real-world examples of how businesses have both succeeded and failed on Facebook, underscoring the treacherous road marketers must navigate while traversing this capricious landscape. Finally at the end of the book, we list assorted Web links that can further enhance your Facebook marketing experience and offer ways that you can protect your identity while in the social network.

Foolish Assumptions

We make a few assumptions about you as the marketer and aspiring Facebook marketing professional:

- ✔ You are 14 years of age or over, which is a Facebook requirement to creating your own profile.

- ✔ You're familiar with basic computer concepts and terms.

- ✔ You have a computer with high-speed Internet access.

- ✔ You have a basic understanding of the Internet.

- ✔ You have permission to perform any of the techniques we discuss for your company.

- ✔ You have permission to use any photos, music, or video of your company to promote it on Facebook.

Conventions Used in This Book

In this book, we stick to a few conventions to help with readability. Whenever you have to enter text, we show it in bold, so it's easy to see. Monofont text denotes an e-mail address or Web site URL. When you see an italicized word, look for its nearby definition as it relates to Facebook. Facebook features — such as Pages and Marketplace — are called out with capital letters. Numbered lists guide you through tasks that must be completed in order from top to bottom; bulleted lists can be read in any order you like (from top to bottom or bottom to top).

Finally, we, the authors, often state our opinions throughout the book. We are avid marketers of the social network medium and hope to serve as reliable marketing tour guides to share objectively our passion for the social network world.

What You Don't Have to Read

- ✔ Don't read supermarket tabloids. They're certain to rot your brain.

- ✔ Depending on your existing knowledge of Facebook, you may want to skip around to the parts and chapters that interest you the most.

- ✔ If you have a good working knowledge of Facebook, you can skip Part I.

- ✔ If you want to set up a Page for your business, go directly to Chapter 4.

✔ If you have a Page for your business and are interested in advertising and promoting it, go directly to Part III.

✔ And if you have a Page and want to start going viral with your marketing, go directly to Part IV.

How This Book is Organized

We organized this book into five parts. Each part, and chapter, is modular, so you can jump around from one to another as needed. Each chapter provides practical marketing techniques and tactics that you can use to promote your business, brand, product, organization, artist, or public figure in the Facebook community. Each chapter includes step-by-step instructions that can help you jump-start your Facebook presence.

Part 1: Getting Started on Facebook

Are you ready to get your company started on Facebook? Before you can answer that question, you have much to consider. Part I talks about what to keep in mind when it comes to Facebook marketing, such as how and why to build a presence on the social network, what the changing demographics in Facebook mean to you, how to become a Facebook member and navigate through the system, and how to expand your business network in the community. You need to make a subtle mind shift along the way that we can only describe as being more open and transparent. Many companies struggle with this, but those that embrace it go on to have a new level of relationships with their customers and prospects.

Part II: Putting Facebook to Work

All marketers — young and old — are looking for ways to put Facebook to work for their companies, small businesses, or clients. In this part, we show you how to secure a spot for your business on Facebook, how to design a great Page, and how to create a strategy for marketing that Page on Facebook. We discuss what it means to market your Page virally, the differences between Facebook Groups and Facebook Pages, as well as how to throw an event in Facebook.

Part III: Strategies for Advertising Success

Part III can help you create a new source of revenue for your business. We tell you how to advertise on Facebook by targeting a specific audience, creating and testing your ads, and then measuring that ad's success. You learn how to optimize an ad campaign and get insights into your customers' interactions with your Facebook Page. And we introduce you to the Facebook Marketplace where you can sell your products and services on Facebook in a way that further promotes your brand.

Part IV: Riding the Facebook Viral Wave

Facebook offers ways to make your presence on Facebook even better! In Part IV, we lead you through a discussion of Facebook applications that you can add or create, and that can help promote your brand. We also discuss how to use Facebook to host a contest and conduct a survey that can give you insights into this ever-expanding Facebook audience. Finally, we show you how to extend the Facebook Platform to your own Web site in a way that further expands the viral marketing effect of Facebook.

Part V: The Part of Tens

We packed these chapters with quick ideas to help you convince others in your company why you should have a Facebook Page, how to conduct yourself on Facebook in a way that best meets your business goals, how to find the latest happenings on Facebook through blogs, and what top business applications you can use on your Facebook Page for business.

Icons Used in This Book

This icon points out technical information that is interesting but not vital to your understanding of the topic being discussed.

This icon points out information that is worth committing to memory.

This icon points out information that could have a negative impact on your Facebook presence or reputation, so please read it!

This icon refers to advice that can help highlight or clarify an important point.

This icon points to Web site locations that complement the text of this book.

Where to Go from Here

If you are new to Facebook and an aspiring Facebook marketer, you may want to start at the beginning and work your way through to the end. A wealth of information sprinkled with practical advice awaits you. Simply turn the page and you're on your way!

If you are already familiar with Facebook and online marketing tactics, then you are in for a real treat. We provide you with the best thinking on how to market on Facebook based, in part, on our own trials and tribulations. You might want to start with Part II, but it wouldn't hurt to take in some of the basics as a reminder and learn about some of the new menus and software features — you are sure to pick up something you didn't know.

If you are already familiar with Facebook and online marketing tactics but short on time (and what marketing professional isn't short on time), you might want to turn to a particular topic that interests you and dive right in. We wrote the book to be modular so you don't need to read it from front to back, although you're certain to gain valuable information from a complete read.

Regardless of how you decide to attack *Facebook Marketing For Dummies*, we're sure that you'll enjoy the journey. If you have specific questions or comments, please feel free to reach out to both of us. We would love to hear your personal anecdotes and suggestions for improving the future revisions of this book. And in the true spirit of sharing on which Facebook is built — we promise to respond to each of your comments.

Here's to your success on Facebook!

Part I
Getting Started on Facebook

The 5th Wave   By Rich Tennant

Tarzan - Lord of the Web

"...and then one day it hit Tarzan, Lord of Jungle – where future in that?"

In this part . . .

Are you ready to market your company on Facebook? Before you can answer that question, you have much to consider. Part I talks about what to keep in mind when it comes to Facebook marketing, such as how and why to build a presence on the social network, what the changing demographics mean to you, how to become a Facebook member and navigate through the system, and how to expand your business network in Facebook. Facebook marketing requires a subtle mind shift along the way that we can only describe as being more open and transparent. Many companies struggle with this, but those that embrace it go on to have new kinds of relationships with their customers and prospects.

Chapter 1

Introducing Facebook Marketing

*1*t's been said that if Facebook were a country, it would be the sixth most populated nation in the world. Imagine being able to get your message in front of the Facebook nation free. That's exactly what Facebook is offering companies with Pages: an online location for businesses, organizations, and individuals looking to market themselves to the Facebook community.

Not just for businesses, Pages can be created by not-for-profit organizations, public figures, entertainers, photographers, and professionals of all types. Facebook Pages are fun and easy to set up, provide a powerful set of online tools for engaging with your customers (or, as they are called in Facebook, *fans*), and easy-to-understand metrics to measure your success.

Every day, 3.5 million people become fans of a Facebook Page, according to eMetric's February. 2009 Facebook Usage Metrics Worldwide study. That's a lot of fans. Although popular consumer brands, such as Apple, Coke, and Skittles enjoy large installed fan bases, smaller brands, business-to-business (B2B) companies, consultants, and personalities can also build a loyal following by using Facebook Pages.

Building a Presence on Facebook

Prior to online social networks, companies centered their Internet strategies on their Web site. Typically, advertisements and promotions focused on driving traffic to that site and success was measured by traffic metrics and conversions, such as how many forms were completed or how many items were purchased. Now, the market is throwing these companies a twist: With the growing popularity of social networks in general, and Facebook in particular, people's online consumption habits are changing. For one, they're spending a lot of time on Facebook. The average Facebook member visits the site an average of nearly 18 times per month, according to recent figures by Web traffic analytics provider comScore.

That's why marketers like you can no longer be content to stay on your .dot-com islands. In response to the challenge, many marketers are adapting their Internet strategies to include these major hubs of social activity by using a mix of advertising, promotional, and word-of-mouth campaigns to drive awareness, traffic, and engagement. And they're interacting with their customers in new and unprecedented ways.

Facebook has remade itself to satisfy marketers' needs to take part in the conversation. They've managed to balance commercialism with its members' strong desire for privacy while fostering an open, transparent environment where discussion flows freely between consumer and marketer.

It's within this new Facebook marketing paradigm that the role of traditional marketing is changing. It's no longer a question of whether your business should have a dedicated marketing presence on Facebook. Now, the only question is do you really need a Web site anymore!

Chasing the Changing Demographic

Look into a mirror sometime: You are the future of Facebook. Young, middle-aged, elderly, male, female, Hispanic, Caucasian, African American, Asian, Indian — no single defining demographic represents Facebook members. If you thought you were too old, guess again. Facebook is experiencing its fastest growth among women 55 and older. Furthermore, teenagers now make up a paltry 12 percent of the Facebook audience. Overall, however, the fastest growing group by total users is still age 26 to 34.

So why are adults flocking to Facebook in droves? Could it be the desire to reconnect with old friends, former co-workers, and family separated by time and distance? That pull is strong within most of us. Or, is it the basic human need to be part of a community, recognized for one's contributions and right to express thyself? One thing's for sure, Facebook is no longer a fad and is not to be ignored by marketers, big or small.

Facebook opened to non-students in May 2006. Since then, Facebook has grown to become much more than a social network. According to Facebook, it is the largest online depository of photos, with more than 850 million images uploaded to the site each month. Additionally, Facebook is available in 35 languages (another 60 languages are promised) with more than 70 percent of users coming from outside the U.S.

The Facebook factor

The astounding growth rate of Facebook continues to amaze. Below are some stats provided by Facebook as of November 2009. For updated stats, visit the Facebook statistics page. Scroll to the bottom of your Facebook screen, click the About link, and at the top of your screen, click the Press tab to access the Latest Statistics link.

General Growth

More than 300 million active users

At least 50% of active users log on to Facebook in any given day

The fastest growing demographic are people 35 years old and older

User Engagement

Average user has 130 friends on the site

Users spend more than 8 billion minutes on Facebook each day (worldwide)

More than 45 million users update their statuses at least once per day

More than 10 million users become fans of Pages each day

Applications

More than 2 billion photos are uploaded to the site each month

More than 14 million videos are uploaded each month

More than 2 billion pieces of content are shared each week

More than 3 million events are created each month

More than 45 million active user groups exist on the site

International Growth

More than 70 translations are available on the site

More than 70% of Facebook users are located outside the United States

Platform

More than one million developers and entrepreneurs from more than 180 countries are creating applications for the Facebook Platform

Every month, more than 70% of Facebook users engage with Platform applications

More than 350,000 active applications are currently available on the Facebook Platform

More than 250 applications have more than one million monthly active users

More than 15,000 Web sites, devices, and applications have implemented Facebook Connect

Mobile

More than 65 million active users who access Facebook through their mobile devices

People who use Facebook via their mobile devices are almost 50% more active on Facebook than non-mobile users

There are more than 180 mobile operators in 60 countries working to deploy Facebook mobile products

Take a closer look at Facebook's recent demographics, as reported by noted Facebook blog, *Inside Facebook,* in February 2009. Clearly, the site's appeal is both broad and growing, highlighted by the following:

✔ Facebook is growing in every age and gender demographic. Fastest growing segment: Women over age 55, up 175 percent over the previous 120 days.

✔ Facebook is growing faster with women than men in almost every age group. Women comprise 56 percent of Facebook's audience, up from 54 percent in 2008.

✔ In Facebook, 45 percent of the U.S. audience is now 26 years of age or older.

Facebook offers you the opportunity to get your message to all these demographics for free. What an efficient way to reach out and expand your customer base.

Homesteading on a Facebook Page

Pages are probably the best place for an organization to hang a shingle out on Facebook. Pages serve as a home for business entities — a place to notify people of an upcoming event, provide hours of operation and contact information, show recent news, and even display photos, videos, text, and other types of content. For example, the Skittles Page encourages users to share experiences and memories of Skittles, as shown in Figure 1-1.

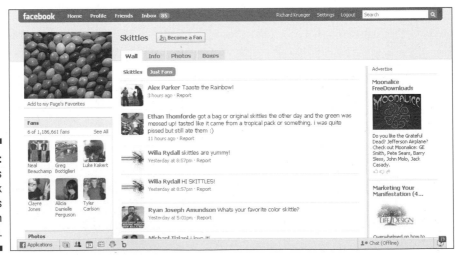

Figure 1-1: The Skittles Facebook Page has more than 600,000 fans.

Pages also allow for two-way conversations between a business and its customers. In this way, Facebook provides a great feedback mechanism to learn about your customers' needs. A Facebook Page is similar to a profile: joining as a fan is similar to becoming a friend of another member. (For more information on personal profiles and Pages, see "Why Create a Facebook Page" later in this chapter.

Facebook Pages are publicly available to everyone, (personal Profiles can also be made available to public search engines via Search Engine Privacy Settings as seen in Chapter 3), regardless of whether the viewer is a Facebook member or not. This last point is important because public availability of Facebook Pages means that search engines, such as Google, can find and index these pages, often improving a company's positioning in search results.

So, let's look at some of the ways that Pages can help you promote your business on Facebook.

Wall

The Wall tab serves as the central component of a Facebook Page and is similar to your personal profile. The Wall allows your company and your fans to upload content, such as photos, videos, and notes. These actions generate updates (called *stories* on Facebook) and often display as stories on your fans' News Feeds.

News Feed

A News Feed displays these stories and publishes any new social actions that take place on your Page. For example, an addition of a new photo to your Page is reported as a story on your News Feed.

Status updates

If a company wants to push out a message, the addition of status updates is a welcome tool in the Facebook marketer's toolbox. Like in personal profiles, Pages allow you, a Page administrator (*admin* in Facebook), to send a limitless stream of updates (short messages up to 160 characters in length), which, in turn, appear in your fans' News Feeds.

Discussions

Discussions are another standard feature that allow anyone to create a new topic of conversation and permit follow-up comments. (See Figure 1-2.) Members can add to any discussion by typing their comments in the appropriate box and clicking the Post Reply button.

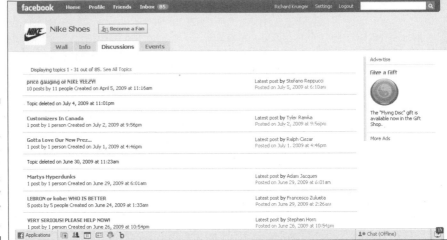

Figure 1-2:
Facebook Pages feature discussions that allow two-way interaction.

Applications

Just like a profile, you can customize a Page with a host of applications (*apps*). Not all Facebook apps work on a Page, but a wide range of useful apps are available ranging from virtual business cards to RSS feeds from your favorite blogs and news services. (See Figure 1-3.) (To find out more about Facebook apps, see Chapter 12.)

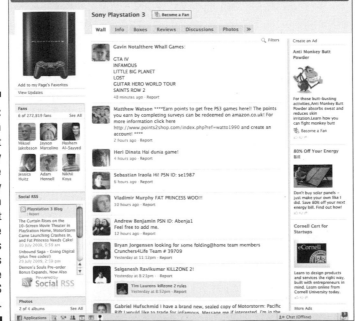

Figure 1-3:
Pages can also sport third-party apps, like this Sony PlayStation 3 Page that features the company's blog posts via the Social RSS app.

If you want to view a directory of Facebook apps that can enhance your business Page, you can choose Applications⇨Browse More Applications on the bottom left navigation bar. In this new Facebook apps directory, click Business in the left column to list relevant apps for your Page. (Alternately, you can get to the Application Directory by going to www.facebook.com/home.php?#/apps/index.php.)

When creating a Facebook Page, use only those elements that either provide value to the visitor or represent the brand in a positive, audience-appropriate way.

Who Uses Facebook Pages?

Facebook Pages are for public figures, businesses, and brands who want to establish a presence on Facebook and start interacting with fans. Pages can be enhanced with apps and provide an open forum for discussions and shared content. Only the official representative of the artist or business controls their Facebook Page. (For more information, see Chapter 4.)

Facebook Pages provide a great opportunity for both business-to-consumer (B2C) and business-to-business (B2B) marketers to get the word out about their product or organization. Here are some examples of companies who use Facebook now.

Benefits for business-to-consumer marketers

Business-to-consumer (B2C) marketers were quick to realize the value of Facebook as a branding opportunity. Entertainment companies, such as movie studios, book publishers, and music labels, were among the initial advertisers on Facebook and that continue to have a major presence.

Although well-known brands, such as Coke, Nutella, and Pringles attract millions of fans to their Facebook Pages, there are also more esoteric brands, such as Marshmallow Peeps (shown in Figure 1-4) and Bacon Salt, that are leveraging their Facebook Pages to drive engagement with customers and build interest in their products. Their marketing strategies take advantage of the viral power of Facebook, relying on fan participation to generate a stream of News Feed stories, which in turn creates word-of-mouth awareness and funnels new fans to the Page.

The challenge is giving people a reason to participate. Whether it's sharing hilarious pictures of Peeps in compromising situations or debating the benefits of salt and bacon as an essential part of a diet, consumer-facing businesses are interacting with their customers in entirely new ways via Facebook.

Here are the main reasons every B2C marketer needs to have a presence on Facebook:

✔ Facebook offers consumer marketers an excellent brand-building environment, thanks to its viral marketing capabilities.

✔ Facebook allows companies to interact with their customers to gain valuable consumer insights.

✔ A Facebook Page improves a company's search engine rankings.

Benefits for business-to-business marketers

Consumer marketers aren't the only ones to benefit by having a presence on Facebook. Many B2B (business to business) marketers are also tapping into the social network's business appeal by reaching out to their customer base where they live and play. From accounting firms like Ernst & Young, who launched a targeted recruitment advertising campaign to attract recent CPA graduates, to technology management consultancy BearingPoint, who sponsored a contest for best "Green Enterprise" idea, B2B marketers are leveraging Facebook's community-oriented tools in exciting ways.

And why are they on Facebook? Because that's where their customers are. For many B2B marketers (for example, see BearingPoint in Figure 1-5), Facebook is another touch point, a new channel from which to communicate directly with their customers, partners, and employees — past, present, and future.

Figure 1-5:
B2B
companies
use
Facebook to
build brand
awareness.

Many of the same benefits that B2C marketers enjoy on Facebook apply to the B2B world. From community building to providing a customer feedback loop to search engine positioning, Facebook helps build relationships regardless of whether an organization is selling to businesses or individuals.

Here are the main reasons every B2B marketer needs to have a presence on Facebook:

✔ Companies are leveraging Facebook as a recruitment tool by reaching out and promoting positions via the Facebook Marketplace (see Chapter 11), industry-related groups within Facebook (see Chapter 7), and highly targeted Facebook advertising campaigns (see Chapter 9).

✔ B2B marketers are using Facebook as a feedback loop, giving the customers a forum where their voice can be heard and appreciated.

✔ Facebook offers B2B companies with disparate offices a centralized online hub to interact, share knowledge, and facilitate employee communications.

Why Create a Facebook Page?

Both personal profiles and Pages have gone through several transitions and the distinctions between the two continue to blur. Capabilities once found only on profiles, such as status updates, the News Feed, and the Wall are finding their way onto Pages. These feature upgrades all serve to the marketer's advantage. (To create your own Facebook page, see Chapter 4.)

Pages versus personal profiles

Each Facebook member has a unique personal profile on Facebook (Figure 1-6 shows an example of a personal profile.) An individual can have only one profile per email account and that profile can only be created, maintained, and credited to that person. Often, people create both a personal profile and a more public profile using separate e-mail addresses.

A Facebook member can have multiple Pages, but only Pages created by the real public figure, artist, brand, or organization, or by an official representative of the entity. Pages are managed by admins, whose names are never revealed. You are the admin for your Page unless you specify someone else.

Finally, Facebook Pages have no fan limit, and can automatically accept fan requests, whereas profiles are restricted to a 5,000-friend limit and friends must be approved.

Figure 1-6:
Every Facebook member has a profile.

Using a personal account for promoting business interests, or creating an unauthorized Page, may result in a warning or even an account termination. So, be safe, use your profile page for personal networking and your Page for business promotion.

Pages versus Groups

Only an official representative of a business, public figure, nonprofit organization, artist, or public personality can create a Page and serve as its admin. Pages are designed to provide basic information and feature community building blocks, such as discussion boards and the ability to comment, upload user-generated content, and post reviews.

By contrast, any members can create a Facebook Group about any topic — and they do. Groups serve as a central hub for members to share opinions and discussions about that topic. Whereas Pages allow for a high degree of interaction and rich media with the addition of applications, Facebook Groups do not allow for the addition of applications.

When an admin updates a Group page (see Figure 1-7), the News Feed story includes the name of the group's admin. Pages, however, attribute updates to the Page and never reveal the admin's name. Groups also don't offer the status update capability, which has recently been added to Pages.

Figure 1-7: A Facebook Group provides members with an online hub to share opinions about a topic.

Group admins can send messages to the entire group's individual Inboxes, provided the group has fewer than 5,000 members. Page admins, however, can't send messages to all members. Group admins also have the ability to restrict member access by requiring a member approval process, whereas Pages can only restrict members from becoming a fan by age and location requirements. For example, alcohol and cigarette companies are prohibited from marketing themselves to minors and so restrict fans who are below legal age limits.

To create a Group, choose Applications⇨Groups in the bottom left navigation bar, and then click the Create a New Group button.

Chapter 2

Joining the Facebook Community

Facebook is all about making connections. Whether it be reuniting with old high school chums, or meeting new people with similar interests, Facebook provides a framework that makes it easy to discover, reach out, and share with others. Smart marketers are discovering ways to attract and grow their network of Facebook clients, known as *fans* in the Facebook universe, to achieve their objectives.

But before you can market to Facebook members, you need to be part of the Facebook community. Facebook offers plenty of opportunities for organizations to get exposure, many available for free. But, before you can create a Facebook Page, start your own Facebook Group, run a Facebook ad campaign, build a Facebook application, or sell your wares on the Facebook Marketplace, you need to be a Facebook member. So, if you haven't already taken the plunge, what are you waiting for?

So, What Took You So Long?

If you're like many people, perhaps you thought (or still think) that Facebook wasn't for you. That Facebook is all about fun and games and flirting and preteen angst, which has no value as a business tool. Or that only bad things could come from sharing your thoughts, pictures, likes, and dislikes for the entire world to see.

Or, perhaps your children's protests sounded the loudest warning, bringing both trepidation and a feeling of being so out of touch with technology that you'd be rejected, denounced, or publicly drawn and quartered by the *digeteria* (a cute name for the digital elite).

But now, after all your belly-aching, procrastinating, and gnashing of your teeth, you've decided to join Facebook and see for yourself what the fuss is about and how it may help to expand your business. It seems a day doesn't go by when you don't read something about the Web's newest phenomenon, or worse, receive an invitation to join from a friend or work associate. And although you might be familiar with professional online networks, such as LinkedIn or Xing, you've so far resisted the lure of Facebook.

After all, you're resourceful, a true professional with real business acumen. Relax, you can figure this out. If 250 million people have already discovered and joined Facebook, how hard can it be?

Networking in Facebook

If you imagine a map representing all of your relationships and then expand it to include the external relationships of each of those contacts, you get an idea of the concept behind a social network such as Facebook. When you connect with folks through the Facebook confirmation process, it's as though you're inviting them into your circle.

Whether you're representing yourself, a business, a nonprofit organization, a polka band, or a political cause, in Facebook, just like in the real world, your ability to form strong relationships and influence your fans determines your ultimate success or failure in achieving your objectives (that is, getting what you want).

Engaging with your fans

Facebook wasn't the first online social network, but has arguably done the best job in providing its members a safe, social environment in which their actions (for example, posting a photo album), if they so choose, can be automatically broadcast as news stories to those friends who are interested in reading it.

Businesses are now realizing the value of being part of Facebook to engage their fan base. It's this viral capability, or ability to broadcast actions as news stories, that has helped fuel the growth of Facebook and makes it an ideal environment from which to market to other members.

Embracing openness

Although no man is an island, Facebook is making it harder and harder to live in anonymity. That's why there needs to be an implicit, trusted, symbiotic relationship with people in your circle of friends. Your Facebook friends' actions might very well end up on your Facebook profile, and similarly, your actions could end up on their profile. This trade-off between privacy and openness is difficult to balance for most new members, not to mention marketers looking to leverage social media.

To some extent, Facebook requires a new mindset based on the concept of openness. Facebook marketers need to embrace openness, while understanding the inevitable challenges and pitfalls that go along with it. Unlike previous mass media (such as, print, radio, and television), Facebook is a two-way medium, lending itself to a new kind of relationship between consumer and marketer — a relationship based on trust, openness, and transparency.

It's important to note that there is a major generational shift in the amount of information people disclose via online social networks. The younger generation (teens and college students) has much less fear and trepidation of broadcasting their lives, warts and all, via Facebook, YouTube, Twitter, blogs, and other social media, whereas those who didn't grow up with the Internet are typically much more hesitant to release even the slightest bit of information.

Since the lines are blurring between many people's professional and personal lives, you need to realize that business relationships may in fact crossover and become part of your Facebook personal network of friends. But that doesn't mean your entire life or business needs to be an open book. Basic common-sense rules that apply while on Facebook include:

- ✔ Only disclose information that you're okay making publicly available.
- ✔ Don't be nasty or offensive because you never know who will read your post.
- ✔ Never reveal personal details that you might regret later.
- ✔ Never publish your contact information.

Whether you're commenting on a photo or writing how you feel as a status update, the information that you disclose is not necessarily a private conversation. Openness has its risks and consequences, so you have to decide where you draw the line.

Getting Started on Facebook

Now that you've glimpsed how Facebook can be a great marketing tool for your business, you need to sign up and start using this social networking tool. You'll then be on your way to joining, creating a profile, uploading your photos, and finding friends for fun and profit.

Facebook often changes its Web site without prior notice. Some of the features in this chapter might appear slightly different from what we describe at the time we published this book. Please note that we strive to be as current and accurate as possible.

Joining Facebook

To sign up for your own Facebook account, all you need is a valid e-mail address.

Businesses can create their own dedicated presence on Facebook (see Chapter 4), but you still need to be a Facebook member to access much of the site, use its features, and interact with other members.

Follow these easy steps to register with Facebook:

1. **Open your Internet browser and go to www.facebook.com.**

   The Facebook welcome screen appears, as shown in Figure 2-1.

Figure 2-1: The welcome screen allows for easy sign-up.

2. **In the Sign Up section, type your First Name and Last Name in the name fields.**

3. **Type your e-mail address in the Your Email address field.**

   Facebook sends a confirmation e-mail to this e-mail address, which completes your sign up process.

4. **Type a password in the New Password field.**

5. **Select your sex in the I Am drop-down box.**

6. **Select your birth date in the Birthday drop-down boxes.**

   Please note, birth date is required to ensure that all members comply with age requirements. Often, members who do not care to share their actual birthday use Jan. 1 in the date field. Also, Facebook gives you the option of hiding your date-of-birth year, to shield your actual age.

7. **Click the Sign Up button.**

   After you click Sign Up, the Security Check feature appears, as shown in Figure 2-2.

8. **Type the *captcha* that you see in the Security Check section.**

   A captcha is a security feature in which you need to enter the exact phrase you see on the screen.

9. **Click the Sign Up button again.**

10. **In your confirmation e-mail, click the link to authenticate your membership.**

    Congratulations! You are now officially a Facebook member — one in a community of more than 250 million people around the globe.

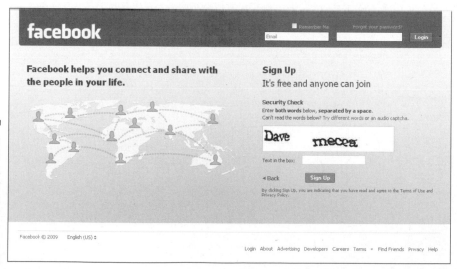

Figure 2-2:
The Facebook Security Check feature for member registration.

Creating a personal profile

Facebook tries to make filling out your profile information as painless as possible with a simple, three-step process. You can choose to enter as much or as little information as you desire.

Although your protective side may be telling you not to reveal anything about your personal history, it's important to note that by adding this information, you're making it easier for people you may know to find you. However, the eventual number of contacts you add as friends and the amount of information that you disclose is entirely up to you.

For example, by not listing your high school, you won't be included in search results for that particular school; therefore, you're invisible to classmates who might be looking for you. Likewise, by not adding previous companies that you worked for, past associates looking to reconnect with you will have a harder time discovering your whereabouts.

 Providing personal information on this page is not mandatory; you can simply skip these questions by clicking the Skip this step link in the lower-right corner of the shaded box. If your goal is to sign up as a business member to create a business Page, then follow this simple three-step process, and head to Chapter 4.

 Only disclose information that you're comfortable having publicly available. This goes for profile questions on political views, religion, relationship status, as well as for age, sex, and home neighborhood. Don't ever post unsavory or compromising photos as your profile picture, or anywhere within Facebook. Your actions are transmitted to others in the form of news alerts, so don't do anything that you wouldn't want everyone you're connected with to know. There are too many stories of people losing a job or a job opportunity because of improper images on their Facebook profile pages.

Find friends

After responding to your confirmation e-mail, you are then whisked off to the Find Friends Using Your Email Account page, as shown in Figure 2-3. To find people on Facebook that you already know, use your existing contacts, already stored in your Webmail account (Facebook supports AOL Mail, Microsoft Hotmail, Google Gmail, Yahoo! Mail, and others) and Instant Message account (Facebook supports AIM and Windows Live Messenger). You can then simply select the contacts that you want to *friend* via Facebook.

 If you provide a friend's e-mail address, Facebook stores this information to send invitations and reminders, to register a friend connection if your invitation is accepted, to allow you to see invitations you have sent, and to track the success of its referral program.

Figure 2-3:
Import your
existing
contacts to
reach out
and friend
someone
you know.

Facebook then extends a friend request to those contacts. Contacts that are
existing Facebook members receive a friend request notification on their
Facebook profile page. Contacts who are not registered members receive an
e-mail invite from Facebook.

To prevent someone from finding you on Facebook, search for that person's
name, and click the click the Report/Block Person link on the right side just
below their photo.

Add profile information

Type your education history, work history, and associated years on the Fill
Out Your Profile Info page, shown in Figure 2-4. Yawn! This can take a while!
Click the Save & Continue button when you finish.

Business professionals may want to use the city where their company or
industry is based. For example, many hi-tech professionals outside Northern
California still prefer to list Silicon Valley as their regional network because of
the access it provides to other Silicon Valley members.

Set profile picture

First impressions are everything. Never underestimate the importance of a
good profile picture. Facebook is a visual medium and everyone is interested
in personal appearances. Make your face count on Facebook. And to be sure,
it should be your face — not your pet, your child, your significant other, or,
worse still, the Facebook default image.

To add your profile picture, roll your mouse over the existing Facebook
default image and you see the link prompting you to upload a picture. Click
the link. Notice a pencil icon by your options in Figure 2-5. Whenever you
enter Facebook edit mode, you see this pencil icon.

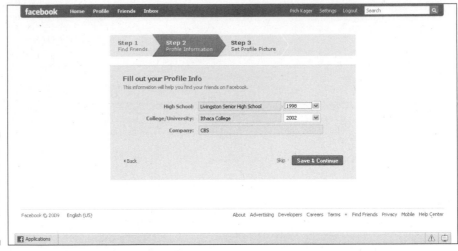

Figure 2-4:
Fill out your profile with education and work history.

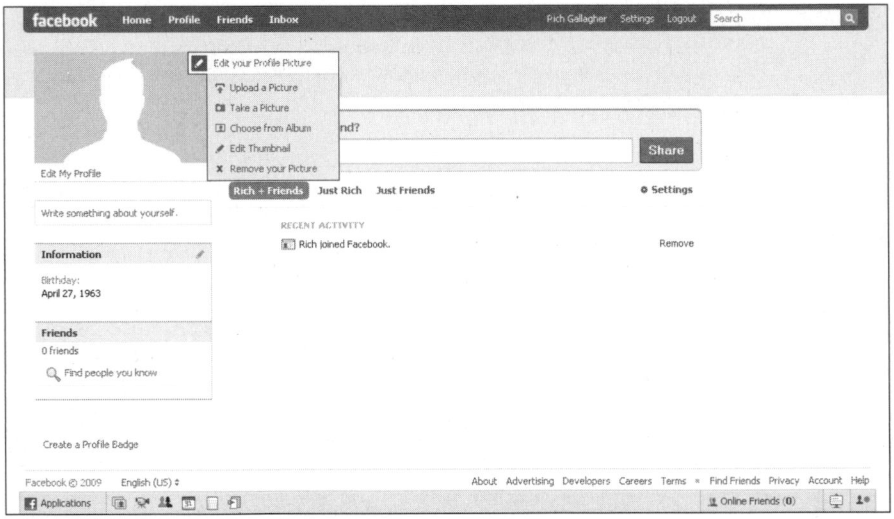

Figure 2-5:
Adding your profile picture is a snap. You can even take it yourself if a digital camera is connected to your computer.

You are then presented with a range of picture options, including:

- ✔ Upload a Picture
- ✔ Take a Picture
- ✔ Choose from Album
- ✔ Edit Thumbnail
- ✔ Remove Your Picture

For first time users, click Upload a Picture to search your computer's hard drive. Select an image file and click Upload. You can upload a JPG, GIF, or PNG file up to a maximum of 4MB. You also have the option to use Facebook's edit, delete, and crop tools. Figure 2-6 shows a rather hip profile photo.

Figure 2-6: You can further adjust your profile photo by clicking Edit Thumbnail.

A neat trick to using larger images is selecting Choose from Album within your profile picture edit menu. You can then select an existing photo that you have previously uploaded to a Facebook photo album, which expands the image to a height of 600 pixels.

If you don't have a suitable image on your hard drive but have an external or built-in camera, you can choose Take a Picture from the profile picture edit menu, which then asks for your permission to allow Facebook's internal Take a Profile Picture application to capture your picture and automatically upload it to your profile.

You can change your profile picture at any time. You can even set up a profile photo album and rotate between those images. After you have a profile photo, you can further refine it by *tagging* the photo, where you attach names to people pictured in the photo. If they're a Facebook friend of yours, they receive a notification that they're tagged in a photo, along with a link back to your picture. See Chapter 6 for more information on tagging.

One of the most compelling yet daunting aspects of Facebook is that each member gets to create his own profile. This is a chance to define yourself via responses to both standard and more esoteric questions, such as Write Something about Yourself. Like you, your profile should be unique, honest, and engaging.

One final note about customizing your Facebook profile. As Shakespeare's Hamlet said, "To thy own self be true." That could just as easily have been written about Facebook profiles in addition to the prince's quest for the truth. Be honest, be transparent, and most of all, *be yourself.*

Logging into Facebook

When you're a Facebook member, you can log in from most computers connected to the Internet.

To log into Facebook, surf over to www.facebook.com and you'll see two entry fields on the top for your e-mail and password. When you log in, use the same e-mail address that you used when registering. Click the Login button and you're immediately taken to your Home page.

If you are on your own computer and want to be remembered on future visits, click the Remember Me check box above the e-mail field. This allows you to avoid the login process and go directly to your Home page when entering the site.

For new members, logging in to Facebook is always a chicken-and-egg-type situation. Without many friends, not many News Feed stories are generated. So, Facebook presents new users with the following options (as seen in Figure 2-7):

- ✔ **Find People You Email**
- ✔ **Find People You Know**
- ✔ **View and Edit Your Profile**

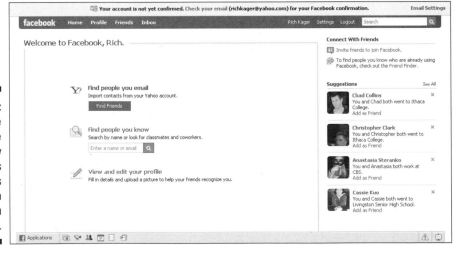

Figure 2-7:
The Home page for new members connects you with people you know.

Finding Friends for Fun and Profit

After becoming a Facebook member and setting up your personal profile, it's time to start making friends. After all, being on Facebook without friends is like being in a forest with no trees. It gets lonely and there's not much to do or see.

Facebook members add connections by *friending* one another. That is, you send a friend request to someone, and the other party confirms that you are indeed a friend before becoming your Facebook friend. If a friend request is rejected, Facebook does not send the person who made the request a rejection notification. When a friend invitation is confirmed, Facebook sends a confirmation notice to your registered e-mail address and posts it to your News Feed and Notifications menu depending on your privacy settings (see Chapter 3).

As you grow your network of friends, this can be a significant asset to your business. By having an opt-in audience, you can leverage your friend-base through comments, updates, and Inbox e-mail. Just like in the real world, having influential friends can benefit you in many ways. You just have to know how to influence the influencers. If you launch a Facebook Page (for more information on building a Page, see Chapter 4), you can transition your friends into fans of your Page through gentle coaxing.

Finding friends

You can find friends and contacts by using several search and import capabilities within Facebook. To start, return to your Home page by clicking the Home tab on your top navigation bar. Facebook displays the Find People You Know link in the center of this page. Click this link and Facebook displays all your search and import options, as shown in Figure 2-8.

At the bottom left of the screen, you see the Find Former High School Classmates, Find Current or Past College Classmates, and Find Current or Past Coworkers links. These tools are useful in tracking down old friends, family, and associates. There's also a default search box for searching via name or e-mail address.

Drill into each of the search functions a little deeper to get a sense of the search options available. For example, with the classmate searches you can add the class year(s) that you attended or graduated from a particular school, or leave the year fields blank to return the widest possible matches. By experimenting with narrowing and widening the results, you can discover many close contacts, familiar names, and old friends long forgotten. Figure 2-9 shows a search for friends using the school search feature.

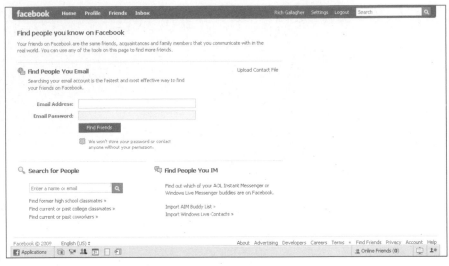

Figure 2-8:
Facebook
provides
tools to
help you
discover
contacts
and grow
your friend
base.

Figure 2-9:
Looking
for friends
using
Facebook's
Search
page.

It's up to you who to friend. If you receive a friend request from someone, you don't have to accept it. If you don't actually know the person or have any friends in common, a good rule of thumb is not to accept the request, unless your goal is to expand your network no matter what. You can find all outstanding friend requests on your Home page. If you want to accept the request, simply click Confirm. If you don't want to accept the request, click Ignore.

After you identify a Facebook member worthy of your friendship, you can extend a friend request by clicking the Add as Friend link to the right of that person's name within the search results. You also find these other links: Send a Message, View Friends, and View Friends in Common (if any). It's always a good rule of thumb to send a personal message when friending folks so they have a point of reference when they receive your friend request. Typically, they'll reply with a friendly message back.

By viewing a person's friends, you can get a good sense of his network, which might then lead you to discover additional friends. This *social graph* is how people tap into friends of friends in an effort to expand their own network. Facebook even shows you friends that overlap with the Friends in Common view. Click this link to see which friends you have in common. After all, a social network can be thought of as circles that intersect at certain points. Or, six degrees of you!

You can also send a friend request from within someone's profile page. Simply visit their profile and click the Add *(name)* as a Friend link directly under their profile photo. ***Note:*** Because you're not already friends, you only have access to profiles of members with a common network, depending on their privacy settings.

By clicking this link, a friend request is sent to the person and you receive notification if the request is accepted. Additionally, you can also choose Send a Message or Poke without having to be a friend. If you *poke* someone, they receive notification that they are being poked by you the next time they log in to Facebook. It's a gentle way to let someone know that you're thinking of him or her.

Creating friend lists

After you have a healthy number of friends, Facebook lets you organize your gaggle into lists, or groups, with its Lists feature. For example, you can create a work list that consists of co-workers or business contacts. Lists allow you to quickly view friends by type and send messages to an entire list. Facebook allows up to 100 lists with up to 1,500 friends per list. (See Figure 2-10.)

To create a list, click Friends at the top of any Facebook page. On the Friends page that appears, click Make a New List on the left. Type a title for your list. You can add friends to your list by typing your friend's name into the Add to List field. You can also click Select Multiple Friends to the right of the field, which allows you to select numerous friends from your entire list. After making your selections, click Save List to store your changes.

If you have more than two lists, click the Expand box next to a friend from the Friends page to quickly add that friend to any of your lists.

Figure 2-10:
Organizing
friends into
lists allows
you to send
a message
to an
entire list.

You can contact a list from within your Inbox. Entering the name of your list into the To box allows you to send a message to everyone on the list. When you select the list you desire, the list expands to show all members of the list; the title of your list is never visible to other members of Facebook. So, if you put a bunch of geeks in a list and name it "Geeks," they'll never know you classified them as such. Another advantage is that you can create separate privacy settings for each list. See Chapter 6 for more on Facebook settings.

Chapter 3

Finding Your Way Around

● ●

● ●

The Facebook evolution has been a bumpy road. Two major upgrades in the past two years were met with a tremendous outpouring of opinion and debate. The most recent upgrade, which went live in March 2009, resulted in the company capitulating to member demands, giving users greater control over the ability to filter the flow of stories.

The company's much anticipated upgrade also moved the News Feed stories — a dynamically updated, real-time view of your friends' social activities on Facebook— to the Home page. Stories often include links that lead you to a photo album, a video, a Facebook Group that you can join (see Chapter 7), or a Facebook Page for your business (see Chapter 4) that you can connect to. This continuous stream of news keeps you informed of your friend's activities and draws comparisons to Twitter, another fast rising social network. Dubbed by many as the *twitterization* effect, the design underscores the potential of the social graph stream. No one knows where this stream leads, but one thing is for sure, the Facebook News Feed is the heart and soul of the beast that is Facebook.

The Home Page

The Facebook top and bottom navigational toolbars offer an iconic design with easy access to the site's core functionality. The Home link takes prominent, top-left positioning. Figure 3-1 shows a glimpse of a Facebook Home page as of this writing. Home is where you land after signing in to Facebook, and you can easily arrive there from anywhere in Facebook by clicking the Home link on the top navigation bar. The Home page features a three-column format, which we describe in the following sections.

Figure 3-1:
A typical
Facebook
member's
Home page.

 Facebook often changes its Web site without prior notice. Some of the features in this chapter might appear slightly different from what we describe at the time we published this book. Please note that we strive to be as current and accurate as possible.

The center column

Facebook's Home starting point offers a Live Feed, highlighting your friends' social actions as they occur. It also offers a News Feed, which aggregates the most interesting content that your friends are posting. The What's on your mind? box (known as the Publisher in Facebook) takes a top-center position, and is where you can update your status by posting messages, photos, notes, links, and more. These posts also show on your profile (on the Wall tab) and on your friends' News Feeds and Live Feeds. Your News Feed or Live Feed is displayed below the Publisher. You can control how much information you want to receive and exactly whose activities you see in your feeds. To the right of every feed story, you can click the Hide link to stop viewing that friend's feeds. (For more information on generating News Feed stories, see Chapter 6).

News Feed

Facebook uses the News Feed to deliver news and information as it relates to you and your friends' activities. News Feed stories are selected based on Facebook's proprietary algorithm that takes into consideration a member's actions on the site, the privacy settings of everyone involved, your interactions, and your account and applications settings. Facebook weighs all these elements in deciding which stories to publish for each member. The key is relevancy, which Facebook's News Feed algorithm is very good at delivering.

News Feed stories represent only part of the content created across your social graph (see Figure 3-2). You will not see stories by friends whose privacy settings restrict you from seeing their actions. Likewise, your privacy rules dictate what actions of yours Facebook publishes as news stories on your friend's Home page. Facebook gives you plenty of control over your News Feed stories — from what you receive to what is published about you.

Facebook allows you to prevent certain types of stories from being published about you. To find out more about your Privacy Settings for your News Feed, see "Managing Your Settings," later in this chapter.

News Feed stories do not display any actions or content that your friends normally are not allowed to see. For example, if you post a photo album and only allow specific lists to view that photo album and a certain subset of your friends are not included in that list, they will not receive a News Feed story about this action.

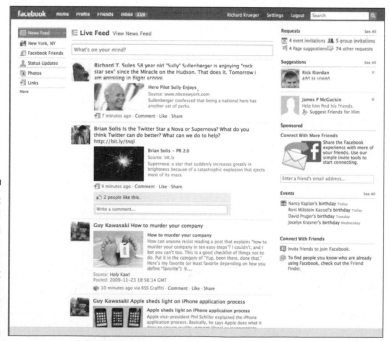

Figure 3-2:
Live Feed
displays
stories in
real time;
more recent
stories
appear at
the top.

Status updates

The What's on your mind? box is where you can share your content, whether it be text, photos, video, notes, music, and a whole lot more. (See Figure 3-3.) The question "What's on your mind?" is displayed inside the status update box and you can address the question directly by sharing text messages up to 160 characters that appear in your friends' (or, for business Pages, *fans*) News Feeds. (See Chapter 6).

To update your status and post your message, click in the What's on your mind? box at the top of your screen. Type the text that you want to share (and/or attach a photo, video, or Web link), and then click the blue Share button.

Figure 3-3:
Personal profiles and Pages offer the ability to send status updates.

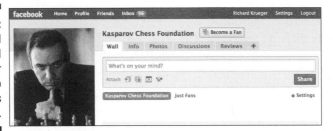

For both your personal profile and your Page, you have to be extra careful when sharing with others. Whether it be a message, a photo, a link, or videos, if your friends (or fans for Pages) find your updates boring and irrelevant, they'll hide you from appearing in their News Feeds. An inappropriate update could result in a drop in fans. So, it's always good to follow some basic rules when posting updates on behalf of your personal or professional use.

Following are a few status updates do's and don'ts that can help keep your fans engaged:

Status updates do's

Always remember when updating your status to keep your content fresh.

Make an effort to post updates on a regular and ongoing basis.

Post relevant statements and questions to your fan base to encourage participation.

Be up front with your posts, which speaks to a company's willingness to be open and transparent with fans.

Include URLs to drive traffic to appropriate information and resources.

If you want to include a link, use a URL shortening service, such as TinyURL.com or bit.ly, to condense the length of a URL. Bit.ly (`http://bit.ly`) can even provide stats on how many people actually click through to the page.

Status updates don'ts

Never make the following mistakes that can make your Page feel like a distraction.

Don't make updates that are irrelevant to your audience.

Don't send an over abundance of updates. It no doubt turns off your fan base and dilutes any newsworthy updates.

Don't be too personal. Your Page's sole purpose is to promote your business, not to update fans on your personal life.

Don't use a hard-sell approach in your updates. Over-aggressive marketing may result in fan revolt.

Don't use updates to broadcast frivolous, mundane, or inconsequential information.

The left column

The left column provides a set of filters that allow you to limit information in your News Feed by using lists. You can also display only application-related stories, stories with photos, stories about Facebook business Pages that interest you, and so on. Facebook is giving its users a lot of control in determining what types of stories they want to receive and by whom.

The right column

The right column displays information regarding any outstanding requests (event invitations, friend requests, group invitations, and even news updates). It also displays suggestions for friends, based on an advanced algorithm that infers connections between members. If you click the photo or *see friends* link, you're taken to a page of 20 or so profile pictures of suggested friends. When looking to expand your friends network, this is a good feature to explore.

We recommend that you only friend, or accept a friend request from, people you know or folks who are at least friends of friends.

The Highlights section provides an added stream of updated news stories, albeit in an abbreviated format. Typically, there's an emphasis on recently updated videos and photos within this section. Farther down the column are Events, which includes friends' birthdays, and then Connect with Friends, which includes the Invite Friends to Join Facebook link and the Friend Finder search page link.

The Top Navigation Toolbar

Facebook conveniently places its most important functions in a toolbar at the top of your screen. The top navigation features primary links, which include: Home, Profile, Friends, Inbox, your name, Settings, and Logout. (For information on the Home page, see "The Home Page" section earlier in this chapter.) The Facebook Search box is at the end of the toolbar and is the quickest way to find people, Pages, Groups, Events, and so on. In this section, we introduce you to each of these key features and what they can do for you.

Profile

Next to the Home link, the Profile link shows you the screen that others see when they visit your personal profile. It displays the most recent News Feed update at the top of the screen right next to your name. Just below are the recently updated Facebook feature called tabs that display Wall, Info, Photos, and more. These tabs help organize your content and allow for easier viewing of your profile information.

It's important to spend some time completing your personal profile, even from a business perspective, as business and personal often blur on Facebook. Plus, Facebook allows profiles to be indexed by the major search engines, so more and more, your Profile is becoming your public face on the Web.

And since creating a Facebook Page (see Chapter 4) starts with your personal profile, take this opportunity to really position your business. Try to make your profile something that is remarkable to the reader. Do you do something really well, better than anyone? Do you make the best deep dish pizza in all of Greenwich? Why not position yourself as an expert on the topic with which you most want your business to be associated?

Wall

The Wall is the central focus of your profile and features continuously updated information (see Figure 3-4). Facebook's Wall allows you to post messages, links to other Web pages, photos, or videos via the What's on your mind? box beneath your tabs. When you make Wall posts, News Feed stories are generated and published on your Wall and in your friends' News Feeds.

When visitors see these stories, often they take other actions, such as visiting a photo album or installing a particular application. The viral nature of Facebook News Feeds serves to promote the post, causing more people to take interest in the posted action.

From your friends' status updates to updates from business Pages for which you are the admin or fan, to your friends' interactions, such as uploading a photo, every story that is being generated by you, about you, or by your friends, appears on your Wall. You can also filter the stream of stories by displaying only stories generated by you, stories about you generated by your friends, or both.

Likewise, you can view your friends' activities by visiting their Wall. It's no coincidence that the Wall is the first page you see when you visit a friend's profile and vice-versa. It represents a member's social interactions — what you do on Facebook, and increasingly, what you do when you're not on Facebook, thanks to Facebook Connect, which extends many of the Facebook features to external Web sites. (Read more about Facebook Connect in Chapter 15.)

Figure 3-4:
The Wall tab found on your personal profile page shows all of your recent activity, as well as that of your friends.

Info

Clicking the Info tab from within a profile takes you to personal information that can help identify you. This is information that won't likely change that often, such as your primary network, sex, birthday, hometown, relationship status, political views, and so on, as well as contact information, interests, and education and work histories. The more information you provide about yourself during registration or while editing your profile, the more information that will display. (See Figure 3-5.)

The Info tab is also a great resource when business prospecting. If you identify someone with whom you want to do business with, you can find out a lot about them from the information detailed within their Info section.

In the left column are your profile picture, brief information about you, your friends, and recent links to friends' photo albums.

Figure 3-5:
The Info tab on a personal profile shows a member's basic information, contact information, and associated Facebook Groups and Pages.

Photos

Next to the Info tab, the Photos tab displays all the photos posted by you, the photos posted of you by others (if any), and any photo albums that you've created. Facebook is home to more than 12 billion photos, making it the largest photo site in the world by a good distance. According to Internet traffic measurement firm comScore, nearly 70 percent of the Facebook monthly visitors either view or upload photos (See Figure 3-6). For more detailed information on adding photos and videos to your Facebook Page, see Chapter 6.

Figure 3-6:
The Photos tab shows pictures featuring or shared by a member.

Friends

Connecting with old and new friends is a major part of the Facebook experience. Facebook makes it easy to find friends. Pointing to the Friends link, which is next to the Profile link in the top navigation toolbar, Facebook displays a pop-up menu that shows the Recently Added, All Friends, Invite Friends, and Find Friends links. Or, you can simply click Friends to be taken to the All Friends page. (See Figure 3-7.)

Increasing your number of friends (or fans to your Page) enhances your network, giving you a large audience from which to connect. Reach out and friend/fan someone and add value to your network and your brand.

You can control what information is available to your friends, including your contact information. You don't have to share your telephone number or e-mail address with friends. You can choose not to include the information during registration or, if you already have information posted, you can visit your personal profile, click Edit My Profile just below your profile picture in the left column, and delete the information that you do not wish to share. (See Chapter 2 to learn more about Facebook friends.)

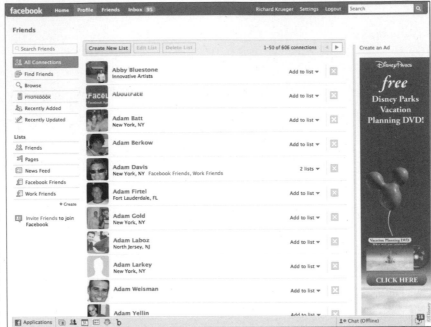

Figure 3-7:
A Facebook
member's
main
Friends
page.

Inbox

Facebook has an internal e-mail system that offers a secure option for communicating with other Facebook members, regardless of whether they're a friend or fan. You can also send an e-mail from your Facebook Inbox to an external e-mail address, simply by typing that e-mail address into the To field.

Mail sent internally via Facebook has a much greater open rate than traditional e-mail. While Facebook does not allow members to spam, or send mass e-mails, to other members, by using the Facebook Inbox for communicating with your business contacts, it stands a greater chance of being read. (See Figure 3-8.)

Your messages are only available to you and there is never a News Feed story associated with your Inbox actions. So, e–mail away without fear that your actions are being published as a news story.

To read your mail, choose Inbox⇨View Message Inbox. A list of four tabs are displayed: Inbox, Sent Messages, Notifications, and Updates.

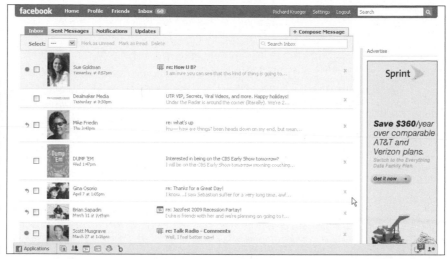

Figure 3-8: The Facebook Inbox allows members to message one another in a private, secure environment.

Hovering your cursor on the Inbox link displays a pop-up menu with the View Message Inbox link and the Compose New Message link. You can also compose a message to a member from the right side of any search results screen.

To send a message, just follow these easy steps:

1. **Choose Compose New Message in the pop-up menu, or click the Compose Message tab at the top right of your Inbox.**

2. **Type the recipient's name.**

   A message box appears.

3. **Type a subject and body to the message, and click the Send button.**

   The recipients are notified the next time they log in to Facebook, and via their regular e-mail address, if their settings permit.

A message can be sent to a maximum of 20 Facebook friends and non-Facebook members. To send to non-members, enter their regular e-mail address. If you're sending to a member who's not a Facebook friend, you can only send to their internal Facebook e-mail, not an outside email address.

The Inbox also features tabs at the top for organizing your e-mails. These include:

- ✔ **Sent Messages:** By clicking Sent Messages, you're presented with all the Facebook e-mails you've sent.

- ✔ **Notifications:** Provides a stream of News Feed stories focused on notifications, such as birthdays, events, and other social actions triggered by you and your friends' interactions on Facebook. You can filter notifications by those you've received and those sent by the result of your actions. (See Figure 3-9.)

    Facebook also alerts you when you receive a new notification with a red notification alert appearing on the bottom right of the chat menu.

- ✔ **Updates:** Offers a News Feed with the latest updates that are generated by the Pages that you're a fan of, Groups that you belong to, as well as applications that you've added. Updates are an ideal way to stay informed about your competitors, customers, and leads. To control which updates you receive, click the Edits Updates Settings on the bottom right side of the Updates page.

You have complete control over what information is published. See the "Settings" section, later in this chapter.

Figure 3-9: You can find recent Facebook notifications on the Inbox link's Notifications tab.

RSS Feeds are an integral tool for today's business professionals, providing a streamlined method for receiving a constant stream of information. To create an RSS Feed for your Facebook Notifications, go to your Inbox and click the Notifications tab. On the screen that appears, you see the Subscribe to Notifications section in the right column. By clicking the Your Notifications link, an RSS Feed automatically generates that you can cut and paste directly into your RSS Reader. You're updated RSS Feed now alerts you to all your Facebook notifications as they happen.

Your name

Your name displays as a link on the top navigation bar on the right side. If you click your name, it takes you to your personal profile. It's of paramount importance that your profile projects your voice, whether you're marketing yourself or a business. Your personal settings can help filter your persona from the public's view. As personal and professional worlds often collide, it's best to create some walls of separation between the two.

Settings

The Settings link is next to your name, and is where you can set all your privacy and account preferences. When you hover your cursor on Settings, a pop-up menu appears with the following options:

- ✔ **Account Settings:** You can change key information associated with your account, such as how you want your name to display to changing your contact, password, networks, notifications, mobile, and language settings. You can also enter or change credit card information if you choose to send gifts or purchase ads, and deactivate your account if you desire. Keep in mind, the account information you choose to show represents you, so choose your networks wisely and simplify the stream of notifications you receive and publish for others to see. (See Figure 3-10.)

- ✔ **Privacy Settings:** All your privacy settings, grouped by Profile, Search, News Feed and Wall, and Applications, are controlled here. Facebook allows a wide-range of choice when it comes to setting your privacy settings. From allowing everyone to view your profile to customizing access to just a few friends, you can choose what and with whom to share. (See Figure 3-11.)

TIP

To control who can access your personal profile from the Privacy Settings options, click the Profile link. From the Profile drop-down menu, choose either Everyone, My Networks, Friends of Friends, Only Friends, or Customized to select from your list of friends specifically.

✔ **Application Settings:** You can edit your application settings, including what information an application publishes on your profile, your News Feed, and your Wall, as well as who can see it (see Figure 3-12). You can add the application to your bookmarks, allow the application to access your data, and set additional permissions depending on the application. (See Chapter 12 for more information about Facebook applications.)

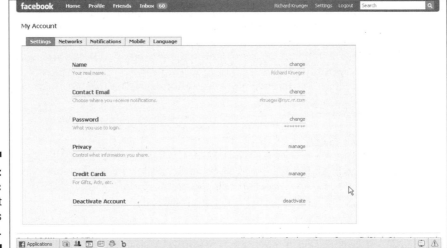

Figure 3-10: The basic Account Settings information.

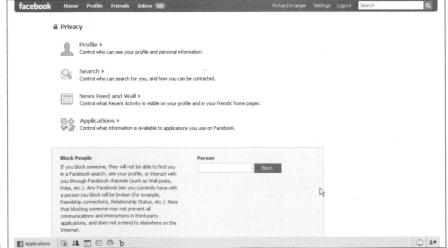

Figure 3-11: All your Facebook privacy settings can be adjusted.

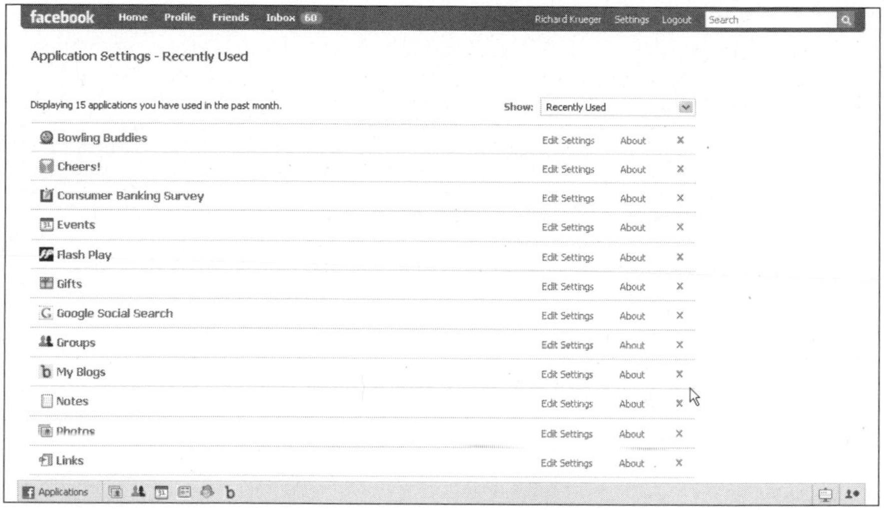

Figure 3-12:
Control
the stream
of stories
regarding
your
interactions
with
applications.

Log out

The last link on the right of the top navigation bar, Logout, is how you sign off from your Facebook account. Clicking Logout redirects the page to the Facebook welcome screen, where you can log in again by entering your e-mail address and password and then clicking the Login button.

It's important to log out at the end of your session so you don't compromise your account access.

Search box

The search box on the top navigation bar allows you to search for names of people, companies, groups, and applications from a single text box. Simply type your search term and click the magnifying lens icon to the right of the search box.

Facebook lets you narrow your search results, choosing filters for People (names), Pages (companies, non-profits, public figures, and so on), Groups, Events, or general Web search results provided by the Microsoft Live.com. You can also join a Group, become a fan of a Page, or add someone as a friend from the search results. (See Figure 3-13.)

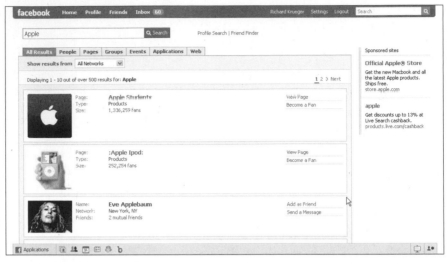

For our example, if you're looking for the Facebook Page about World Chess Champion Garry Kasparov's Foundation, you can search for any part of the name to find the Page listed in the results. You can enter 'Kasparov', as well as 'Chess' or 'Foundation' and it shows up in the results. If you are interested in chess, you might be interested in finding related Groups. You can search for 'educational games', or 'board games' to yield some Groups that may be of interest to you. Searching for 'chess' brings results from all over Facebook.

1. **At the top right of your screen, click in the Search box.**

2. **Type a name or title that interests you.**

3. **Click either the image or the name of the Group that you want to visit.**

   In the search results, be sure to note the number of members, the type of Group, and any recent activity, so that you have some indication of how active the Group is before you visit or join.

The Bottom Navigation

The bottom navigation provides convenient access to some of the most powerful features within Facebook. The Applications menu and bookmark icons are on the left and the Chat functions and Notifications are located on the bottom right side.

✔ **Applications:** On the far left side of your screen is the Applications menu, which, when clicked, displays your bookmarked applications. It provides easy access to your Groups, Pages, Events, Links, Notes, Gifts, and more (see Figure 3-14). Facebook Gifts is a real marketplace where members can purchase virtual items to send to other members. (For information on adding Facebook applications, see Chapter 12.)

✔ **Bookmark icons:** To the right of the Applications menu is a list of six icons. Bookmark icons make it easy to access an app at any time by simply clicking the link. Some common icons that Facebook displays include: Photos, Video, Groups, Events, Notes, and Links. These icons change depending on how often you use different applications.

- *Photos:* Takes you to the Photos page. You can view photo albums recently posted by your friends and create a photo album by clicking the Create a Photo Album button. (See Chapter 4.)

- *Video:* Takes you to the Video page where you can view your own and friends' recent video streams. You can also show just your videos, or videos in which you're tagged, via the two tabs on top of the page. (See Chapter 6.)

- *Groups:* Lets you view Groups that your friends have recently joined and Groups you're in. You can also search for groups by using the Search for Groups search box, and create a new group by clicking the Create a New Group button. (See Chapter 7.)

- *Events:* Lets you view your upcoming events, as well as friends' events, past events, and birthdays via the tabs on the Events page. You can also search for events by using the Search for Events search box, and create a new event by clicking the Create an Event button. (See Chapter 8.)

Figure 3-14:
Find bookmarked and recently used applications via the bottom navigation.

- *Notes:* Facebook Notes is a powerful blogging tool that provides Facebook members with a forum to write whatever they choose via the Share box, allowing friends to comment. Similar to tagging a photo, Facebook members mentioned in a note may also be tagged and receive a notification. (See Chapter 6.)

- *Links:* Clicking the posted note icon takes you to the My Friends' Links page where you can view your friends' recently posted links. You post links via the Post a Link text box on the top right of the page. You can sort friends' links by using the drop-down menu to the right or show your own links by clicking My Links near the top of the page. You can even create an RSS feed of your friends' links by clicking My Friends' Links in the Subscribe to Links section in the right column.

✔ **Chat:** Facebook has an internal chat system that allows for instant messaging between friends. This is a great feature for reaching out to your friends in real-time, as opposed to the Inbox e-mail system, or writing on someone's Wall. (See Figure 3-15.)

The Chat feature allows you to change your online/offline status, displays your friends' most recent status update, pop out chat as a separate window, and show News Feed stories in Chat. If your status is set to Online, you see a green dot by the person icon on the bottom navigation bar and the word *Chat.* If your status is set to Offline, the dot appears grey.

Figure 3-15:
Facebook shows the chat status of you and your friends.

Part II
Putting Facebook to Work

The 5th Wave
By Rich Tennant

"Well, it's not quite done. I've animated the gurgling spit sink and the rotating Novocaine syringe, but I still have to add the high-speed whining drill audio track."

In this part . . .

All marketers — whether young or old — are looking for ways to put Facebook to work for their companies, small businesses, or clients. Part II shows you how to secure a Page for your business on Facebook (an important starting point for marketers), design an engaging layout, and customize it to meet your needs. We help you create a strategy to promote your business and show you the various tools and tactics that Facebook offers.

We then discuss how to virally market your Page throughout the Facebook platform and learn the distinctions between Facebook Pages and Facebook Groups. Finally, we show you how to host your own Facebook Event.

Chapter 4

Creating a Page for Your Business

*I*f someone offered you retail space in the heart of Times Square, rent free, would you open a business? Of course, you would. Well, that's exactly what Facebook is doing with Facebook Pages. As a result, hundreds of thousands of businesses have hung their shingle out on the social network.

In this chapter, you learn all about what Facebook Pages are and how to use them for your business. We walk you through creating a business Page and give you tips on how to customize it for optimal effect. We also help you attract customers (that is, *fans* in Facebook) for your business Page, and introduce you to the viral nature of Facebook Page promotion and the Facebook features that can help you.

What Are Facebook Pages?

Facebook Pages give your business a presence on Facebook to promote your organization. Facebook Pages are the business equivalent of a Facebook member's profile. Members can become a fan of your Facebook Page (similar to becoming a friend to your profile), write on your Wall, learn about special promotions, upload photos, and join other members in discussions. And you can share your status updates with your fans to keep them engaged and informed. For more information about Facebook fans, see the "Finding Facebook Fans" section, later in this chapter.

Unlike profiles (where the number of friends is limited to 5,000), Facebook does not limit the number of fans a Page can acquire. A business can send updates to all of their fans at any time. Therefore, think of a fan as an opt-in subscriber, with Facebook providing the infrastructure to reach your fans via Facebook's internal e-mail and Wall features, among others.

Another key difference between Facebook Pages and profiles is that Facebook Pages are public by default. This means that anyone can search and find your Page with the Facebook search engine and with the Internet search engines, such as Google and Yahoo, thereby helping your business gain visibility and broadening your audience beyond just Facebook. To find out more about profiles and Pages, see Chapter 1.

For even more search engine visibility, consider getting a vanity URL on Facebook, which can include your company name in the Facebook Web address.

Facebook Pages found with a search engine are visible to non-Facebook members, but they require the user to join Facebook if they want to interact with the Page, such as make a comment or enter into a discussion.

Facebook Pages also allow you to add *applications* (apps), or small interactive software programs, to your Page to engage your readers further with videos, notes, links, discussions, Flash content, and more. Depending on which category of Facebook Page you choose, you can see that some apps are standard and can't be removed, such as your Wall, Events, and Notes. Facebook also maintains a large library of third-party apps that you can use to make a Facebook Page your own. (See Chapter 12.)

Facebook Pages come in three categories:

- **Local:** Local pages are meant for business that would benefit from a strong local market presence. A breakfast cafe, pizza shop, or an advertising agency is an example.

- **Brand, Product, or Organization:** These pages are meant for larger national businesses, which could include nonprofit organizations or soft drink companies. Starbucks and Coca-Cola are good business-to-consumer examples; Avaya and Oracle are good business-to-business examples.

- **Artist, Band, or Public Figure:** These pages are good for a politician, an artist, or a musical group. Barack Obama or the band Nine Inch Nails are examples.

Exploring Page elements

Good news: Facebook Pages allow for a flexible layout. Some of the Page elements are universal to every Page and come loaded when you create your Page, such as the picture on your Page, the Wall tab, Information tab, and the Events box in the left column. This helps maintain a consistent look across all Facebook Pages. However, you can add new tabs (predefined or custom built) to your tab list, and many elements to your left column, which you can reposition by dragging and dropping the box that outlines each element.

Depending on which category you select when you create your Page, your tab display may vary. For example, if you chose Local⇨Cafe, you see a Reviews tab in your tab list (see Figure 4-1).

Universal Page elements include:

- ✔ **Picture:** When it comes to projecting an image — figuratively and literally — your picture is one of the most important elements of your page. Be sure to choose a good, clear image that best represents your business.

- ✔ **Wall tab:** Another important element when creating conversations for your Wall. Here, you can leave updates about your business and fans, or friends and fans can leave comments that everyone can read.

- ✔ **Info tab:** General info about your company. Fields are category specific to your business: Government businesses ask for parking and hours of operation; fashion businesses ask for Web site, company overview, and mission. These fields can be left blank initially and completed later.

Facebook Pages are public and these fields can help you with the search engine optimization of your page so it is best to fill them in with content that contain keywords you wish to be found under on a search engine.

Figure 4-1: Facebook lets you add any of the following universal tabs, and more.

To add a new tab, click the + sign next to the Info tab. There you'll find a bunch of default Page tabs including:

- ✔ **Photos:** Lets fans tag photos on your Page and notify other fans via a link to view the pictures. This is a fun, key feature because tagging photos spreads the word about your Page. (See Chapter 6 for more information about tagging photos, notes, and videos.)

- ✔ **Events:** Lets you organize events or gatherings with your fans. It also allows you to alert your community about any upcoming events you may be having. (See Chapter 8 to find out how to host an event.)

- ✔ **Notes:** Lets you share happenings in and around your company with your fans. You can also tag fans of your company in notes, so they can leave you comments.

- ✔ **Video:** Provides a high-quality video platform for Pages. You can upload video files, send video from your mobile phone, and record video messages to all your fans. Additional features include full-screen playback, tagging your fans in videos, rotating videos, and more.

- ✔ **Discussions:** Lets your fans express their ideas, questions, and suggestions. Discussions let you know exactly what your fans and customers think and want from your company. Think of this section as a community section.

Designing your Page

Before creating a Facebook Page, give some thought to basic design principles. Although there are always exceptions to the rules, some best practices in Facebook Page design include:

- ✔ **Keep it clean:** Too many elements on the Page can detract attention from the brand. Although some apps are productive and useful, try to keep the number to a minimum.

- ✔ **Keep it fresh:** By continuously updating your Page, you're giving your fans a reason to come back often, which generates social stories that attracts more fans.

- ✔ **Keep on topic:** Your Facebook Page should focus on your business. Although adding RSS feeds and other dynamic content is encouraged, you need to keep it relevant to the business and your fans. As much as you may love Elvis, he doesn't belong on your second-hand jewelry page.

- ✔ **Keep your fans in mind:** Design your Page with your customer in mind. Every element should be of value to them; otherwise, it doesn't belong on your Page.

✔ **Position your company as an authority:** Your Facebook Page signposts your business to the world. This is your chance to show what you know and let your expertise shine.

✔ **Inject some personality into your Page:** Even though a Facebook Page is for business, it should reflect your personality. Find and maintain your company voice throughout your communications. Have fun with it, but convey a professional, quality organization.

✔ **Value feedback:** Facebook, unlike radio and TV, is a two-way medium. Companies shouldn't overlook or ignore the value of feedback received via your Facebook channel. They should encourage it through discussion boards, polls, surveys, contests, user-generated comments and general fan interaction. Feedback is very valuable because so few people actually take the time to give it.

✔ **Fostering a give and take relationship:** Your fans are looking to engage with your Page, but it's a two-way street. It's been written that you must give in order to receive. Make special content available exclusively through Facebook or offer prizes in exchange for feedback — just two ways to show fans that you value their input.

✔ **Generating social stories is key to viral success:** Facebook uses a snazzy sophisticated algorithm to publish social stories that are relevant to like-minded users. You, or your Page administrators (admins), should always be thinking of what social interactions you can perform — or can encourage your fans to perform — to fuel the Wall items.

✔ **General guidelines and limitations:** The Page layout is generally very flexible, but brand guidelines on Facebook must be strictly followed. Any links off Facebook must open a new window. Facebook does not allow pop-ups or pop-unders. The Page cannot be "skinned" with a new background design.

Creating Your Facebook Page

Facebook makes setting up a Page easy. With some basic information about your company, you can get started. To create your Page, follow these steps:

1. **Scroll down to the bottom of your Facebook screen, and click the Advertising link.**

2. **At the top of your screen, click Pages to see the Facebook Pages screen.**

   This contains lots of useful information about business Pages, what they are and how to use them. (See Figure 4-2.)

Create a new Facebook Page

Figure 4-2:
Facebook
Pages
overview
screen.

3. **Click the green Create a Page button in the upper-right corner. (Refer to Figure 4-2.)**

   The process of creating your new Facebook Page begins (see Figure 4-3).

Figure 4-3:
The Create
New
Facebook
Page
screen.

4. **Select the category that best describes your business and choose your business type from the drop-down list.**

   - Local ranges from Automotive to Travel Service.

   - Brand, Product, or Organization ranges from Airline/Ship/Train Station to Web site.

   - Artist, Band, or Public Figure ranges from Actor to Writer.

Choose the correct category from the start because the resulting templates that Facebook generates have different options. For example, if you choose a brand, product, or organization, your Page elements are different from a Local café. The Local café has a section for reviews from your patrons; the brand, product, or organization does not.

For our example, a Web-based tee shirt company that specializes in shirts for toddlers, we selected Brand, Product, or Organization as the category, Fashion as the type of business, and then named the brand, Pop Tot Tees, in the Name of Fashion text box. (See Figure 4-4.)

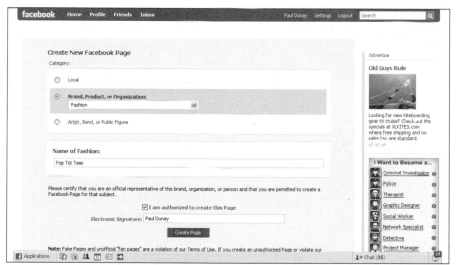

Figure 4-4:
The Pop Tot Tees brand.

5. **Type your business name in the Name of Other Businesses field to secure your company name on Facebook.**

   When you name your Page, it's permanent, so make sure you choose a name that you want your fans and customers to associate with your business. When you get more than 1,000 fans, you can claim a vanity URL on Facebook.

The person who sets up the Page also becomes the default administrator (admin) of the Page.

6. **Click the check box below the name of the page.**

   This makes your page private until you are ready to launch.

7. **Click the Create Page button.**

   By clicking this button, you represent that you are an official representative of the business, organization, entity, or person that is the subject of the Facebook Page — and that you have the necessary rights to create and maintain the Page. Congratulations, you created your Facebook Page!

Your Page will not be live until you click Publish This Page, so feel free to edit it until you think that the Page is perfect. (See Figure 4-5.)

Figure 4-5:
Be sure to
publish your
Page for
others
to see.

⚠ This Page has not been published. To make this Page public, publish this Page.

Customizing your Page

Beyond certain universal elements, Facebook Pages allow you to customize your Page to your liking. For example to change the order of items on the Page, click the item bar and drag it to the desired location. Everything except the photo at the top of the left column is movable, thanks to a very slick technology called AJAX.

AJAX is short for Asynchronous JavaScript and XML, which is a group of interrelated Web development techniques used to create interactive Web apps that users can customize.

Upload a picture

A good place to start is to upload your company logo or a photo of your product. This picture represents you on Facebook so be sure to make it a good one. Or, you can add an animated GIF that has several photos of your product from various angles. If you're a services company, you can have several photos of happy people using your service. You can upload photos in JPG, GIF, or PNG formats only. Pictures can be up to 396 pixels wide with a height three times the width. Maximum file size is 4MB.

To upload the first picture for your Page:

1. **Hover your mouse on the question mark on your screen.**

2. **Click the Change Picture link to view the Edit your Profile Picture dialog box. (See Figure 4-6.)**

3. **Click the Upload a Picture link.**

4. **Browse the picture you are looking for and click Open to start the upload process.**

   You are prompted to write something about the photo, which appears on the Wall of your profile or you can skip that step.

5. **Click Publish.**

Figure 4-6:
Click the
Change
Picture link
to upload a
picture to
your Page.

Info tab

The details of this feature differ based on which category and business type you choose. The Info section has two sections: Basic Info, and Detailed Info.

In this example, we chose the Brand, Product or Organization category to promote our online fashion business, Pop Tot Tees. (See Figure 4-7).

The Info tab content changes depending on which category you choose when you create your Page.

 - **Basic Info:** Enter your basic contact information, such as business address and phone number, as well as hours of operation.
 - **Detailed Info:** Enter more in depth information, as follows:
     - *Web site:* Add your Web site's URL.
     - *Company Overview:* Add your company's boilerplate text on who you are and what you do. Or, you can add content that is more social and less "corporate" to give your Page more personality.
     - *Mission:* Add your mission statement. You don't have to enter one if you don't have one, or you can make up something provocative.
     - *Products:* Add a listing of your products or services. (See Figure 4-8.)

Facebook Pages are public and these fields can help you with the search engine optimization of your page. So, fill them with content that contains the keywords under which you wish to be found on a search engine.

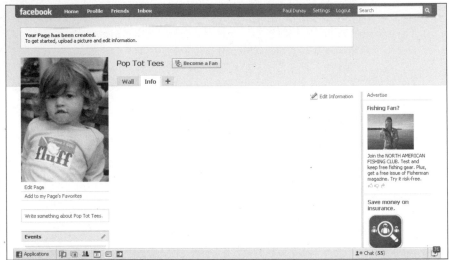

Figure 4-7:
Picture
successfully
uploaded to
your page.

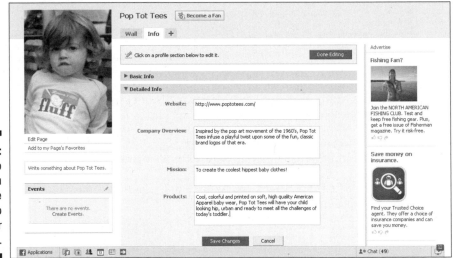

Figure 4-8:
Your Info
tab lets you
provide
detailed info
about your
business.

Wall tab

The Wall on your Page (see Figure 4-9) is where fans of your brand can interact with you, such as leaving a comment, thought, or idea about your company. Also, you can share What's on your mind? as well. Think of this area like a very public message board. You can get creative and use this to post jobs for your company to let people know you are hiring, announce a coming product launch, and gauge interest from your fans.

Figure 4-9:
Your Wall tab is a great place for a welcome message for your visitors.

Your Wall generates and displays stories for anyone who is a fan of your Page. You should keep your Wall active by posting content you already have, such as links to the latest blog post from your company, by using the What's On Your Mind? box. Or, you can add a link to a news item that covers your industry. Here is a list of the items that you can use on your Wall:

- ✔ **Content:** Type a text message up to 365 characters in length. Use this area to discuss anything of interest happening at your company.

- ✔ **Links:** Add any links from your corporate Web site or any news coverage you may get with your fans.

- ✔ **Photos:** Add photos of new products, launch parties, or any photos of people who work at your company. Single photos can be uploaded from your hard drive, taken with a webcam; larger groupings of photos can be made into an album.

- ✔ **Events:** Add an event from your company. You just fill out the Title, Location, and Time and click the Share button.

- ✔ **Videos:** Add a video from your company. You can record a video with a webcam or upload it from your hard drive.

Every time you update the information section of your page, it posts an update on your Wall. Also, anytime you add a discussion using the Discussions tab or write on someone else's Wall, it appears on your Wall. For more information about adding content to your Wall, see Chapter 6.

Photos tab

The Photos tab lets you upload photos for your Page. Use this tab to upload photos that you want to organize in albums to share with your fans. You can also use any photo that you upload as your profile picture, if you want to change it often to keep it fresh.

Facebook also allows you to upload an unlimited number of photos and albums to your Facebook Page. You can reorder photos, rotate them, and acknowledge a Facebook member by "tagging" them in the photo. We explain how to tag a photo in Chapter 6.

To use the Photos tab:

1. **Click the Photos tab.**

2. **Click the Create a Photo Album button.**

   Facebook prompts you for the name of the album, the location of where the pictures were taken, and a short description of the album. (See Figure 4-10.)

3. **Click the Create an Album button.**

   A dialog box opens to help you locate your photos on your hard drive.

4. **Browse on your hard drive to select the photos that you wish to upload.**

5. **Click Upload.**

Discussions tab

Lets you engage your fans to express their ideas, questions, and suggestions. Discussions let you know exactly what your fans and customers think and want from your company. Think of this as a community section. (See Figure 4-11.) For more information, see the "Setting Page access" section, later in this chapter.

To use the Discussions tab:

1. **Click the Discussions tab.**

2. **Click Start a New Topic.**

3. **Type a title for the topic and the content of the post.**

4. **Click Post New Topic.**

Because discussions can grow to contain many topics, Facebook provides you with a topic view so you can see the entire discussion. Find the topic you want, and then click the topic name to see the complete topic view and reply to any comments.

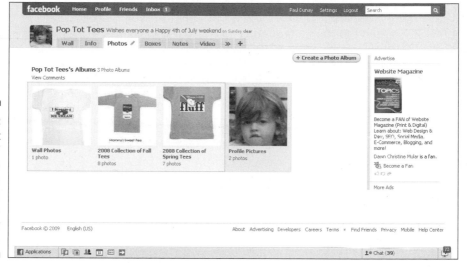

Figure 4-10:
Pop Tot Tees' albums help organize their tee shirts for easy access.

Figure 4-11:
Using Discussions to get some new design ideas from our fans.

Page controls on the left column

Facebook provides links on the left column to help you control your Page. The links in this column represent quick ideas for how to build your audience. No matter which category or type of business you choose, this column preloads with the following items:

- ✔ **Edit Page:** Lets you make changes to your Page by editing your security settings, changing your Wall settings, and activating your mobile settings so you can update your Page from your mobile phone. You can also locate and choose new apps, such as Polls, that you can add to your Boxes tab. (See Chapter 14 to find out how to use Polls.)

- ✔ **Promote Page with an Ad:** Link to the Facebook advertising app where you can advertise your Page on Facebook in three easy steps. Members can become a fan of your Page right from the ad or click through to visit your Page. (See Chapter 9 to advertise on Facebook.)

- ✔ **Active Mobile Status Updates:** This link lets you update the status of your Page remotely with your mobile phone. You choose your country and your carrier. Click Next and you get a code that allows you to send a text message directly to your Page.

- ✔ **Promote with a Fan Box:** Lets you take your Facebook Page and create a widget that you can use on your Web site; thereby giving your Web users a taste of your Page without having to be on Facebook. All you have to do is just copy and paste the code into your Web site template! Note that this feature is visible only after you publish your Page.

- ✔ **Add to My Page's Favorites:** Lets you add a Page to your favorites list. It also generates an item on your Wall for others to see. Note that this feature is only visible after your Page is published.

- ✔ **Suggest to Friends:** Use your friends to build your fan base. Click the photo of one of your friends or type a name in the Search box. Facebook sends them an invitation to join your Page.

- ✔ **Write Something About:** Type a short blurb or mission statement about your company, so people know why you exist or what your mission for the Page is.

Setting Page access

Now that you have almost completed your Page, you might want to limit access certain readers have to your Page before you go live. Facebook allows you to restrict access to your Facebook Page by country: US, Canada, UK, Australia, and several others. You can also restrict access by age: Anyone (13+), People over 17, People over 18, People over 19, People over 21, Legal Drinking Age. Restricting by age is something you may want to consider if you are a local bar or perhaps a tobacco brand. (See Figure 4-12.)

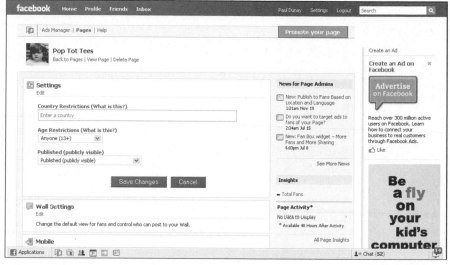

Figure 4-12:
Select
which
countries
have access
to your
Page.

To access your Page settings:

1. **Click the Edit page link under the picture on your Page.**

2. **Click the Edit link in the Settings bar.**

3. **Click Edit to expand the settings.**

   Select the best settings for your page.

4. **Click the Save Changes button.**

Facebook also lets you control what users can do on your Wall. The screen is broken into two parts: View Settings and Fan Permissions. The View Settings is where you can direct new fans to a specific tab. Perhaps you have a video you want them all to see. Otherwise, consider sending them to the Wall by default, or to your company Info tab. (See Chapter 9 for more about landing pages.)

You can also restrict whether fans can write on the Wall or post photos, videos, or links. Our advice is to allow as much interaction as you can with your fans so be sure to check these boxes. (See Figure 4-13.)

To access your Wall settings:

1. **Click the Edit Page link under the picture on your page.**

2. **Click the Edit link in the Wall bar.**

3. **Click Edit to expand the settings.**

4. **Choose the best View settings and Fan permissions for your Page.**

5. **Click Save Changes.**

To publish your page, click the Publish this Page link in the top banner (see Figure 4-14).

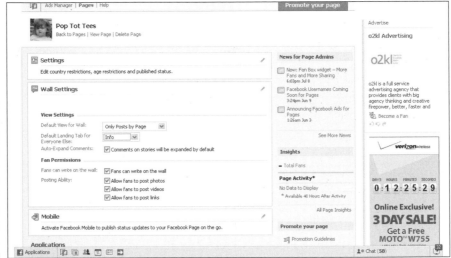

Figure 4-13: Sending new fans to our company's Info tab, rather than to the Wall (by default).

Figure 4-14: Remember to publish your page.

Finding Fans for Your Page

In Facebook, members become a fan of your Page, which gives your business access to millions of possible clients. In fact, more than 5 million fans are added to Pages every week. Pages say something about the celebrities, products, or brands that they endorse. A Page can have an unlimited number of fans, as opposed to personal profiles that are limited to no more than 5,000 friends. (See Chapter 2 to learn how best to populate your personal profile.)

Becoming a fan is easy. When members discover your Page, they can simply click the Become a Fan link at the top of your Page next to your Page name to be added to your list of fans. Their friends see that they've become a fan of your Page in their News Feed, and the fans' profiles show a message that they've become a fan. Fans can also choose to receive messages from your Page automatically to stay connected with your organization.

You should feel free to invite your friends to become a fan of your Page. Facebook offers several features that lets you promote your Page to prospective fans and customers. (See Chapter 6.) Facebook members can also discover your Page on their own and the public can see your Facebook Page when using the Internet search engines.

Sharing your Page

What's a Page worth if you don't share it? Facebook makes it easy for you, or your fans, to share your Page with other members to help you attract more fans. First, you can simply post a message with a link to your Page to your personal profile.

Then, all Pages feature a + Share button in the lower-left column that gives you a choice to either send a message to up to 20 Facebook friends or to post a message about the Page to your profile. (See Chapter 6.)

The Send a Message feature lets you send an e-mail message to a Facebook friend asking them to become a fan of your new Page. Start by letting people know you're on Facebook. You can use your new Facebook Page as a reason to reach out to existing customers, friends, and contacts outside of Facebook through your normal marketing channels. For example, you can send them an e-mail blast or include the Page address in a printed newsletter or flyer. Something as simple as "Join us on Facebook!" does the trick.

Letting fans find you

Facebook members can find your Page in several ways. You can also refer to Chapter 6 for more information on promoting your Page to learn more about Facebook marketing tactics.

- ✓ **Name search:** Members can search for a Page by using the Search box in the top-right corner of your screen anywhere within Facebook. Simply type the name of a company, local business, or public figure, and then click the Search button. Your Page name appears near the top of the search results when a user enters an exact match. (For more information, see "Finding Pages on Facebook" later in this chapter.)

- ✓ **Member profiles:** Profile Walls list each of the Pages friends are fans of. Members can click your Page title in a friend's profile to go to your Page.

- ✓ **News Feeds:** When members become fans of a Facebook Page, stories are published in their News Feeds in their profiles. Members can click your Page title that's embedded within a story to visit your Page.

- ✓ **Public view:** Facebook Pages are available to the public, not just Facebook members, via Internet search engines. Internet users can find links to your Page within search engine results, as well as on Web sites and blogs.

Viral Marketing with Pages

If you build a Page, will they come? Not if nobody knows about it! The same viral elements that have helped make Facebook profiles so popular are also hard at work behind Facebook Pages. No, we're not talking nasty viruses; we're talking a way of spreading your reach. When fans interact with your Facebook Page, their actions become social stories and publish to their News Feeds.

Your friends may very well see these social stories when they log into Facebook and be influenced to take a similar action. The stories link to your Facebook Page, generate social interactions in the News Feeds of their friends, and drive more traffic to your Page. This is leveraging each person's social graph. Meaning through Facebook, users can discover new Pages of interest to them.

Your job is to create actions that generate social stories. Understanding the types of social actions that trigger social stories is key to harnessing Facebook's social graph.

How can you market your Page?

Your goal is to create interaction on your page that gets noticed. To do that you can use a variety of tactics. In this section, we discuss some ideas for sharing, adding features, and commenting. (See Chapter 6 for more information.)

Adding applications

One simple idea is to add apps to your page. By doing so you generate another story on your Wall and in the News Feed of your fans. Facebook has a variety of apps for businesses, entertainment, games, sports, and utilities. (See Chapter 12.) For example, you can use the SlideShare app to share a PowerPoint presentation with your fans or you can add the birthday calendar app to keep track of your local patrons' special day.

Posting and sharing on a Page

Posting a blog or sharing an interesting article you just read that is related to your business is a great way of generating a story. To do this, simply click the What's on Your Mind? box at the top of your Page. Enter a comment about the blog or article and then add the link by clicking the Attach a Link icon.

Comment on your Page

Comments to members or for your Page show your fans that you're engaged in a dialogue with them and add value to the conversation. If you get comments, be sure to respond to as many of them as you possibly can. Nothing keeps the dialogue going like knowing that someone is listening and responding.

Editing Page info

Editing your Page content is a very simple but often overlooked way to generate an item on your Wall. Although we don't advise that you change your information several times a week, we do encourage you to edit your Page when major events occur.

How can fans market your Page for you?

Fans actions on your Page can also generate stories about your business in the News Feed of their friends. Although they are impossible to control, be aware that these actions count in the eyes of a fan's friends and can seem like an endorsement of your Page.

✔ **Becoming a fan:** Creating a strong fan base is a great way to get the viral equivalent of an endorsement of a fan to all their friends. Growing your fan base should be a top priority for you. (See the earlier section, "Finding Fans for Your Page.")

✔ **Wall posts:** Offers another great way for fans to enter into a discussion on your Page. Wall posts also appear on the News Feeds of all the fan's friends. (See Chapter 6.)

✔ **Photo uploads:** Getting users to share photos of them engaging with your product, brand, or public persona is a great endorsement that's visible to all the fan's friends.

✔ **Tagging friends:** Share photos that include the friends of your fans. Be sure to take as many high quality photos at events so you can share them and tag as many people as you can whether or not they are fans of your page. (See Chapter 6.)

✔ **Video uploads:** Add a great sense of interactivity with videos to promote your brand. Running a contest to get members to send in videos is a great way to market your product. (See Chapter 13.)

✔ **Event RSVPs:** Invite your fans to join an online or face-to-face event as another great touch point to consider. Any event you hold should be posted to your Facebook Page. When members RSVP, a new item generates in their News Feed for all their friends to see, perhaps enticing them to come to the event as well. (See Chapter 8.)

Finding Pages on Facebook

When looking for a specific Page on Facebook, the Search box on the top navigation bar is a handy way to find what you're looking for. Here's a quick step-by-step guide to finding a specific Page:

1. **Type the name of the company, product, or personality in the Search box, and click Enter.**

   You're presented with the closest matches in the search results.

2. **If you don't see what you were searching for in the results, click the Pages tab just above the results.**

   Only Pages that closely match the search term display. If you don't see the company, product, or personality, it's most likely because a Page doesn't exist.

Facebook also provides directories to help you find Pages of several types, as shown in Figure 4-15. Facebook Pages are divided by major categories, including Places, Products, Services, Stores, and so on.

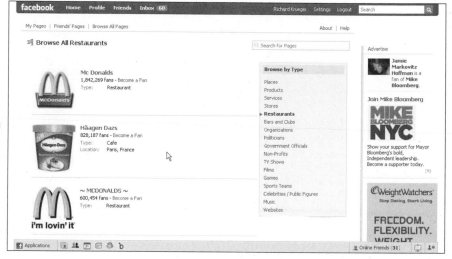

Figure 4-15:
Browsing by
Page type
helps you
find your
favorite
Pages.

Here's how you get to where you can browse Pages by type:

1. **Click the Profile link on the top navigation bar.**

2. **Click the Info tab.**

3. **Scroll down to the Pages section, and click the See All link.**

4. **From the Your Pages page that appears, click Browse All Pages.**

    Using the Browse by Type box allows you to list Pages within catego-
    rized results. Pages with the most fans are featured on the top of the list-
    ings in descending fan order.

For a list of Facebook company directories, please visit us on the Web at www.
dummies.com/go/facebookmarketingfd

Chapter 5

Developing a Facebook Marketing Plan

*O*ne of the great things about Facebook is that it provides you access to a very large and growing audience at relatively low or even no cost. All you need is just a little sweat equity on your part. But that doesn't mean you shouldn't have a strategy for what you are trying to achieve for your business.

Whether you're a small business, an artist or celebrity, or sell a well known (or soon to be well known) product or service, you need to think about your audience, who they are, how they want to be spoken to, what they want, as well as what message you want them to receive and the Facebook tactics that get them to interact with that message.

Traditional marketing — advertising or "shouting at" your customers to get them to buy something — does not work in a social network such as Facebook. It might even work against you. Social networks represent a shift in the way that you use the Internet. Rather than just searching for information, you can search for and interact with like-minded people who have similar interests.

So, approaching your social network marketing with a word of mouth or viral marketing mentality is important. Viral marketing is a way of using customers to promote awareness of your business. One way to think about Facebook for the marketer is that it makes viral marketing simpler. From becoming a fan of a company's Page (see Chapter 4), to confirming attendance at a Facebook Event (see Chapter 8), to installing an application (app) on your Page (see Chapter 12), these social actions are automatically turned into stories that appear on a member's Wall. This exposure to other Facebook members expands word-of-mouth awareness of your business. For more information about viral marketing and your business Page (see Chapter 6).

You are entering into a conversation between you and your customer, so always think in terms of what they want and how they want to be treated. As long as you keep these two things in mind, you'll be successful.

By the end of this chapter, you'll be able to meet these challenges and begin to put your marketing strategy in place. So, let's start with defining your audience.

Defining Your Audience

Whatever your business goals, always assemble the best information that you can about your audience. The better you understand the culture and viewpoint of your audience, the more effectively you can capture their attention and deliver your message.

Unlike Google, which only uses keywords search terms, Facebook can use all of the profile information that member has entered at its disposal. For example, if you are looking to reach men ages 35 - 45 who live in the Northeast and like Scuba Diving, you can do that. With Facebook advertising options (see Chapter 9), you see how to target your message by location, age, relationship status, and interests. You can even specify a language, as Facebook is available in more than 640 languages with many more in development. So, no matter whom you are targeting, Facebook has you covered.

Targeting your demographic

Identifying and then reaching a specific audience has never been this exact and cost-effective until now. The Facebook Insight tool helps you find out more about who is visiting your Facebook Page (see Chapter 10), including an age and sex breakdown of your fans. And the Facebook ad targeting capabilities (see Chapter 9) makes it relatively easy to get your message to the right demographic within Facebook.

The face of the average Facebook user has actually shifted over the past few years. While the Facebook population continues to grow, its total users have started to represent the world's population more closely. But right now, Facebook is in the middle of a shift from a college crowd demographic to a more eclectic one.

The fastest growing demographic is the 35–54 year olds, which have a growth rate of 276 percent. The next fastest growing demographic is the over 55 crowd, which has a growth rate of 194 percent. The core of the Facebook audience, the 25–34 year old group, is still doubling every six months. Moreover, the largest demographic concentration, the college crowd of 18–24 year olds, is down from 54 percent six months ago to 41 percent. And somewhat surprising, more females (58 percent) than males (42 percent) are on Facebook.

Targeting your psychographic (Eek!)

Before you go running for the hills, that's *psychographic,* not psychopathic. Psychographic variables are any qualities relating to a user's personality, values, attitudes, interests, or lifestyles (such as music you love, politicians you endorse, or causes you support). These variables are in contrast with *demographic* variables (such as age and gender) and *behavioral* variables (such as usage rate or loyalty) and can help you target potential customers.

Psychographics is exceptionally relevant in any discussion of social networks because your target audience is more likely to interact with you along the lines of their interests, their values, and the substance of their lifestyle.

Examples of this can be seen in Facebook apps similar to iLike, which integrates your favorite music and makes recommendations on your profile. President Barack Obama's Facebook group was very popular because he tapped into the values of many Americans. Thus, his group grew virally.

Understanding the lives of your customers and prospects is key when communicating your business or product to them. So, let's define a few objectives of your marketing strategy.

Defining Your Marketing Goals

Now that you have a better understanding of the makeup of the Facebook audience and some knowledge of demographics and psychographics of the Facebook audience, you can define a few goals for your Facebook marketing strategy.

Your Facebook approach should at least include these four objectives:

- ✔ Building your brand's awareness
- ✔ Driving your sales
- ✔ Forming a community of people who share your values
- ✔ Listening to feedback about your brand

We discuss each objective in more depth. But keep in mind that they aren't mutually exclusive but rather a combination. You can start with one method and advance your strategy in other areas while you go along.

Building the ultimate brand

The concept of branding can be traced back in history to the early Romans. But the story that always stuck with me was the concept of farmers branding their cattle with branding irons so they could be recognized by the farmer. It was a way of distinguishing their product from other products that looked very similar.

These days things are very similar. A brand is how you define your business in a way that differentiates you from your competition. It is a key element in defining your marketing goals. With a Facebook Page, for example (see Chapter 4), you can build awareness of your brand with all your current and future potential customers.

Pages are probably the best place for an organization to start on Facebook. They serve as a home for business entities on Facebook — a place to notify people of an upcoming event, provide hours of operation and contact information, show recent news, and even display photos, videos, text, and other types of content.

They also allow for two-way conversations between a business and its customers. In this way, Facebook provides a great feedback loop to learn about your customers' needs. A business Page is similar to a personal profile as joining them as a fan is similar to that of becoming a friend of another member.

Start by letting people know you are on Facebook. You can use your new Facebook Page as a reason to reach out to existing customers, friends, and contacts outside of Facebook through your normal marketing channels. For example, you can send them an e-mail blast or include the Page address in a printed newsletter or flyer. Something as simple as "Join us on Facebook!" does the trick.

Within Facebook, you can also send an e-mail to your existing fans or friends with the name of your Page. (Please be aware of the Facebook policy on sending spam.) Plus, Facebook offers a great utility for sharing your new Page — the Share button. (See Chapter 6.)

The Share button, found at the lower left column of any Page, allows you to invite Facebook friends, or a list of Facebook friends, to check out your Page. Plus, you can input an e-mail address of someone who may not be on Facebook so that they can view your Page.

Driving sales

Whether you're a local, national, or international business, Facebook can help you to drive the sales of your products and services. As another potential sales channel, you can leverage the social network in a number of ways to achieve your sales objectives.

Facebook Pages are an ideal way to communicate special offerings and discounts and can provide an easy path to purchase with a simple link back to your company Web site. Some larger retailers are bringing the entire shopping cart experience to Facebook. For example, 1-800-Flowers recently launched a flower store within their Facebook Page. It's easily accessible from a tab (see Chapter 6) labeled Store and provides a secure transaction environment for Facebook members to make a credit card purchase and send a dozen roses to a friend in the real world.

Many marketers are also discovering the potential in Facebook as a cost-effective advertising medium. They're testing and launching targeted ad campaigns that employ traditional direct marketing techniques. The most successful offer is an incentive that appeals to your respective audience. Some brave new marketers are even experimenting with the new video engagement ads to provide a multimedia sizzle to their sales pitch.

The Facebook Marketplace is also a good outpost if you have a business that deals in books, furniture, electronics, cars, tickets, or other tangible items. See Chapter 11 for a discussion of the Facebook Marketplace.

Facebook Events are another avenue from which to drive your sales. For example, you can hold a new product launch party or a wine tasting for potential new customers. And you can throw a Facebook-only Event for fans and allow them to network as well. See Chapter 8 for a discussion of Facebook Events.

Forming a community

One of the best uses of a social network is to build community. No matter what your marketing goals, forming a community can be tricky. We tend to think it arrogant for marketers to feel they can build a community that people will flock to — the proverbial "build it and they will come" model.

It is possible, however, with both Facebook Groups (see Chapter 7) and Facebook Pages for your business (see Chapter 4). You can create a new community focused on an existing cause that matches with your business goals, and gives your group members the tools to communicate with each other in Facebook. (For a comparison of Facebook Groups and Facebook Pages, see Chapter 7).

For example, build a Facebook Group around a cause related to your brand. Lee Jeans' National Denim Day supports breast cancer awareness and the search for a cure — a good cause, and who doesn't like to wear denim! The Lee Jeans' National Denim Day cause informs the Facebook community about wearing jeans to support breast cancer awareness, as shown in Figure 5-1.

Spirited discussions are prominent in Facebook Groups so plan for someone in your company — a product expert or someone on the communications team — to lead regular discussion threads. This could be weekly, bi-monthly, or even monthly. You probably want people coming back to the group more often than monthly but less often than weekly. For example, weekly updates from your Group might be too much for your fans to handle, but because of the nature of the Web, you'll want to remind them to come back to your site more often than monthly just to keep your group fresh in their minds.

Listening to feedback

Facebook Groups gives you the opportunity to create community and have discussions with the members of your Group. But another noteworthy byproduct of forming a Facebook Group is the ability to get feedback from the members.

Next time you think of launching a new product or service, consider having the members of your Group weigh in on it long before it goes to market. And don't worry about a delay getting the product to market; it only takes a few days to get feedback from your member, but you have to build up your member base before you can tap into it. See Chapter 7 for more information about building a Group for your business.

Suppose you are looking for discussions about your brand. Facebook is fertile ground for open, honest peer-to-peer discussions about your business. Just plug any search terms into the Facebook Search box and see what comes up. You might be surprised to find other fan Pages devoted to your brand started by fanatics of your brand.

Facebook does not publish Group discussions to Internet search engines. Therefore, they are not indexed, which is how a search engine finds its information. This may change, but currently there is no way to monitor Facebook Groups via the Internet because they exist behind a password-protected community. So be sure you manually search for your business on Facebook to ensure you see any conversations and feedback.

Facebook Pages are publicly available to everyone regardless of whether the reader is a Facebook member. This last point is important, as public availability of Facebook Pages means that search engines, such as Google, can find and index these pages, often improving a company's search results positioning.

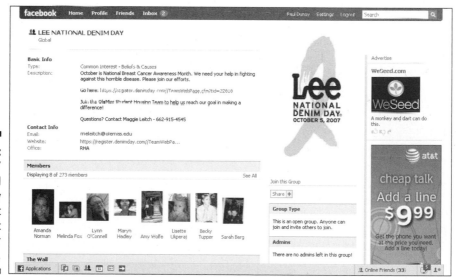

Figure 5-1:
Lee Jeans'
National
Denim Day
to support
breast
cancer
awareness.

Crafting Your Message

Keep in mind when thinking about your business on Facebook that you are entering into an online conversation. So a traditional command and control message won't work.

An example of a command and control message is Nike's *Just Do It,* which is their ever popular tag line. If you search for *Nike* in Facebook, you'll notice that the most popular Nike site (Nike – Just do it) is not owned by Nike (see Figure 5-2). This is a real shift for marketers today — in the past we would have notified our legal department and shut the site down. Now we revel in the fact that we have Pages or Groups devoted to our brand that we don't have to update.

This exemplifies the spirit of Facebook and the way marketers on Facebook need to think. The question quickly becomes: What can you do to help these brand evangelists? Can you invite them to private screenings of your new movie, song, or video? Or, can you give them product to test before anyone on the market?

Figure 5-2:
One of
Nike's most
popular
Pages,
which is not
owned by
Nike.

The culture of Facebook was formed by young, digitally fluent adults who understand when they are being talked at (or commanded to Just Do something) versus engaging in a conversation. So, the key is not to interrupt them with messages, but to use the Facebook features to attract them to your message. By creating a steady stream of rich content, you can engage the right audience and get them to interact with your brand.

Discovering your voice

"Ahem." (Cough.) "La la la la la la la."

Not that kind of voice. Marketers often talk about understanding the voice of the customer, what the customer values, but nowhere is this more important than in Facebook. Because Facebook is ultimately the expressions of its members, it makes sense to hear their needs before listening to the needs of the marketer's business. Ultimately your voice is determined by your customers.

If you want to build trust and have a loyal following on Facebook, you have to become an active member of the community. Start discovering your voice by putting the needs of the community first, building content that gains their trust, and then engaging in honest dialog.

Open versus closed communication

Inside Facebook, the most powerful message is one delivered by one friend to another friend. This means that the marketer needs to ensure that every communication is as open and honest as possible.

Be as authentic as possible and quickly disclose any relationship that could be seen as borderline unethical. A relationship that can work against you undoubtedly will, so be careful.

A very public and notable example of this was a blog called walmartingacross america.com. The issue wasn't that the founders of the blog weren't real brand enthusiasts of Wal-Mart, the issue was that Wal-Mart was paying for them to blog. The relationship was quickly discovered and worked against Wal-Mart. The point here — disclose any relationship that if printed on the front page of the newspaper would make you feel uneasy. This goes beyond Facebook — it's a tenet of all good social behavior!

For more about Facebook Groups, see Chapter 7. We recommend being as open in your communications as possible, which may be more than you are comfortable with. That is okay, however, as that's how it works on social networks. You have to jump in with both feet if you want to run with the crowd.

Applying Your Facebook Marketing Tactics

The toolkit for marketers on Facebook is a little different from the more traditional toolkit that marketers are used to. Advertising has been the traditional path of most marketers. But few marketers are finding that path successful today for a variety of reasons, including the cost of advertising and its effectiveness. Even though advertising is available on social networks like Facebook, it is not a guarantee of success. (See Chapter 9 to advertise on Facebook.)

While Facebook offers advertising as a way to reach out to your customer, it also includes tools that address the more viral nature of the social network. You can maintain a presence on the site (see Chapter 4) and distribute your content (see Chapter 6). To enhance your Page, you can add elaborate software apps (see Chapter 12). Why not hold a contest (see Chapter 13) or host an event (see Chapter 8)?

Presence

Even if you aren't completely ready to market your product or service, get a presence on Facebook. We highly recommend that you reserve your business or brand name before someone else takes it (see Chapter 4 to secure your company name on Facebook).

A Facebook presence, like having a Web site, is a fundamental tactic and should be on everyone's list of must haves. You might want to go ahead and secure your company name on other social sites, too, such as LinkedIn, FriendFeed, Delicious, and Twitter. Similar to the .dot com land grab that happened in the late 90s, secure your company name now for use later.

Advertising

Advertising on Facebook is unlike any other advertising experience you've had because of the unique ways you can precisely target an ad to a specific group of people. For example, if you want to target MBA graduates that are three to five years out of school and working in Southern California that like Rock music and whose favorite food is sushi — you can do that!

Facebook ads work similar to online banner ads, but try not to use them the same way. Most banner ads, when clicked, take you to a completely different site. In Facebook, however, although you can redirect members to your Web site, most users feel more comfortable staying within Facebook — and you want your users to feel comfortable!

Beyond that, Facebook ads are still made up of the basics: an image, some text, and a title. And ads on Facebook are purchased like banner ads, with pay for clicks (CPC) and pay for impressions (CPM) pricing. The big difference is that you can attach social actions to your ads to increase the relevance. Facebook is operating on tons of personal data that users have made available about them on Facebook. So, unlike Google, where you only have keywords to attach your ad to, Facebook makes all aspects of a user's social profile open for targeted ads. (See Chapter 9.)

Applications

Facebook apps can be embedded in any Facebook Page or personal profile to distinguish your profile. You can think of them as interactive spaces that allow the user to get content, take a poll, play a game, or anything else you can dream up.

Creating a Facebook app has become widely popular because custom apps are not that hard or expensive to build. Some Facebook apps have seen tremendous growth because they were built to take advantage of the viral nature of Facebook. And new apps have been built to display advertising, giving birth to a whole new generation of advertising networks.

A great example that was well integrated into the Facebook site was the Fedex – Launch a Package app (see Figure 5-3). The app imitated the real world need to send a package fast, but using the Facebook platform. It was in line with the FedEx brand — simple, fast, and easy to use! See Chapter 12 to learn more about Facebook apps.

Figure 5-3:
Launching
a Package
with the
Fedex
Facebook
application.

Content syndication

Another tactic to consider, if you have a steady stream of content, is to use Facebook as an outpost for your content. If you already have a blog, podcast series, or video series, you can effectively attract your Facebook audience to interact with — therefore displaying — those assets. (See Chapter 6.)

You can syndicate content in a variety of ways on a Page, including:

- ✔ Importing blog posts with Notes
- ✔ Using the My Del.icio.us app to import bookmarks from your Delicious account
- ✔ Using the Simply RSS app to gather all the RSS feeds you're collecting on your company's Web site
- ✔ Editing your Links section to include blogs and Web sites you want to highlight, perhaps by employees or partners of your company
- ✔ Uploading photos, videos, and podcasts (MP3 files) to your Facebook Page

Don't forget to edit your Wall settings to include complete versions of all your blog posts so that they appear not only on your business Page, but also on the News Feeds of all your fans.

Contests

Okay, after you create a presence on Facebook, advertise your company, perhaps create a custom app (or just use existing apps) to dress up your Page, and pull in and syndicate all your content, you might want to kick your marketing campaign up a notch with a contest.

Facebook has no official Contest app, but a few enterprising companies jumped on this opportunity to create their own app to fill the need of marketers wanting to run contests (see Figure 5-4). Contests tap into human nature's competitive tendency and you can use them to help build your fan base, reward an existing fan base, or drive awareness of your brand. (See Chapter 13.)

Figure 5-4:
The Adobe
Real or Fake
Facebook
interactive
game
gained the
company
6,000 new
fans.

Events

Facebook Events are a great way to get people together virtually, or in person, in support of your local business (see Figure 5-5). They are also an economical way of getting the word out beyond your normal in-house marketing list by inviting the fans of your Page or members of your Group. Fans can also help you promote your Facebook Event to their friends by sharing the Event if it seems of value to a group of their friends. (See Chapter 8.)

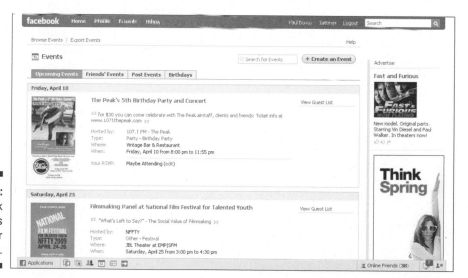

Figure 5-5:
Facebook
Events
manager
screen.

Integrating Your Online and Offline Campaigns

When you start to solidify your strategy, you may question what support systems and resources are needed, or wonder how to integrate your social network marketing strategy with your existing marketing plans. In this section, we make some suggestions on how to support the effort without overloading you or your marketing team, if that applies.

There is no reason you can't leverage your existing offline campaigns with a social network. But be sure you incorporate the campaigns into Facebook the right way. That is, include all elements of your campaign on Facebook. If you are throwing an Event, be sure to mention it on Facebook. If you are starting a campaign, mention it to your Facebook fans. Pretty much anything you are currently doing can be digitized and used on your Facebook Page.

- ✔ Face-to-face events can be promoted. (See Chapter 8.)

- ✔ Advertising campaigns can be adapted and used for Facebook ads. Just be sure to adapt the campaign to be more social and conversational. (See Chapter 9.)

- ✔ Products can be sold in the Facebook Marketplace. (See Chapter 12.)

- ✔ Contests can be adapted to have a social element and drive awareness of your brand. (See Chapter 13.)

- ✔ Research within Facebook can be compared to offline efforts. (See Chapter 14.)

Now you should be ready to get started promoting your Facebook Page (see Chapter 6). If you haven't yet created a Facebook Page, see Chapter 4. Be sure to evaluate your media budget and hire a writer exclusive to your online needs.

Deciding on a media budget

Believe it or not, the cost of the technology used for social network marketing is rather low. For example, a blog costs nothing to start, a podcast can cost up to $2,000, a wiki can cost up to $6,500 per year, and a video can cost up to $15,000. Your own Facebook page is free but a private, branded app on Facebook can cost up to $100,000.

But unlike traditional media — print, TV, and radio — which can cost big money, social networks' upfront costs are very little. A blog or Facebook Page costs nothing to start but the real cost is creating a steady stream of rich content to fill up these new media channels which is where the costs can get large.

We recommend dedicating up to 25 percent of your traditional media budget to non-traditional media. This gives you a healthy budget to experiment with for advertising, apps, contests, and creation of content to be successful in social networks such as Facebook.

Hiring an online writer

To create a steady stream of rich content that attracts the right audience, plan to have access to some additional, perhaps dedicated, writing resource for all your social content needs.

Social writing is a unique skill because the writing needs to be conversational. Headlines need to be provocative and entice the reader into wanting to know more. Above all, body copy needs to have a colloquial tone without a trace of sales or marketing speak.

We recommend hiring a separate writer for social network marketing content unless you happen to be one yourself.

Most people tend to think they can use the same writing resource for research papers, fact sheets, brochures, Web site copy, e-mail copy, and social content. This is a dangerous practice. Having someone who truly understands the medium can help tailor existing content, and writing new content helps to that ensure you always put your best foot forward.

Chapter 6

Promoting Your Page

. . . .

. . . .

*W*here you now tread, many great ones have tread already. Many of today's most popular public figures and commercial products from President Barack Obama to Coca-Cola are already located on Facebook. And scores of other local businesses, brands, actors, politicians, and musicians have done the same. So, there is no reason why you shouldn't create an outpost for your business on Facebook as well.

With a Facebook Page in place (see Chapter 2 to become a Facebook member and Chapter 4 for details on creating a Facebook Page), your attention can turn to building a strong fan base for your Page. Social networking is a quantity game in that the amount of time you spend networking equals the amount of results you receive. For example, if you were to attend a networking event, such as a Chamber of Commerce meeting, you might meet a handful of people. But repeated appearances at these meetings would most certainly build your credibility in the group and your number of contacts.

Think of Facebook, or any social network, in the same way you would the Chamber of Commerce meeting, except the meeting is ongoing and there's no limit to the number of people you can meet (that's a big virtual meeting!). Also, imagine what would happen at the Chamber of Commerce meeting if you walked up to each group of people that you saw, interrupted them, handed them your business card, and asked them to visit your store down the road right now. That approach wouldn't go over very well in that setting, and it won't work for you on Facebook.

In this chapter, we cover a few tactics that are well accepted in the Facebook community that generate conversations rather than interruptions. These tactics help to build awareness of your brand; drive your sales; form a community of people who share your values; and listen to feedback from your customers.

We discuss how to generate the best Wall stories by writing text messages, adding photos and videos, and starting discussions. We show you how to leverage your existing friends and customers both in and out of Facebook, and how to find new business prospects within the Facebook community. Plus, we list seven easy, free ways to market your Page on Facebook that everyone should consider. So let's dive right in!

Positioning Your Page

The way most businesses grow in the offline world is through word of mouth recommendations. You make a good product or provide great service, the word gets out, and customers beat a path to your door. Conversely, if you don't make a good product or provide great service, then customers will avoid you and might never give you a second chance.

Facebook is really no different. In fact, it enhances the word of mouth process because Facebook provides many ways to share Pages and give friends your "digital" endorsement.

The perfect place to start promoting your Facebook Page is with a well-honed position for your brand, product, service, local business, or performer. Try to make your Page something that is remarkable to the reader. Do you do something really well or better than anyone? Do you make the best deep-dish pizza in all of Greenwich? Why not position yourself as an expert on the word you want to get around. (For more information on developing a Facebook marketing plan, see Chapter 5.)

Generating Stories for Your Wall

The core of your Facebook Page is the Wall, where fans can post comments and engage with you in conversations. When a fan posts something to your Wall it shows in their friends' News Feeds, allowing you to keep reaching a wider circle of people. This is the viral nature of Facebook, which is what makes it so powerful!

You can keep your Page engaging and fresh by using simple Facebook features, such as updating your content regularly, adding photos and videos, generating interesting discussions, hosting an event, and more. Here are the Facebook marketing tactics that can make the most of your Page.

Keeping your content fresh

As with so many other forms of social media, the key to a vibrant Facebook Page is fresh content. It can't be any old content, either — it needs to be interesting and relevant content to your readers.

Content truly is king because users who return to your Page regularly are more likely to become customers over the long haul. Moreover, existing customers who return often to your Page are more likely not to leave you, so you owe it to your company to keep the content flowing.

You have several ways to make regular updates:

- **Find content that's relevant to your audience from any content aggregator or blog search engine, such as Digg or Technorati.** By taking the time to search on these sites every day, you can find interesting information to repost so that you can keep your site fresh and keep the conversation rolling.

- **Vary your tactics.** If you find a clever blog post about something you think is relevant to your audience, post it as a status update. For example:

```
Just read this post from ABC on 123. They are on to
    something!
```

- **Find something you don't agree with and post it in your Discussions area to ask your fans what they think about it.** If you see a clever comment in a blog post, for example, you can post the comment to your Wall and add a link to the blog post where you found it.

Adding new messages

Maintaining a steady stream of content helps you to attract new members of the Facebook community, as well as to interact with them. Every time you update the What's On Your Mind? feature, Facebook posts a *story* (a listing of the action that occurred) on your Wall.

Other stories that post on the Wall include starting a discussion, adding a photo, uploading a video, throwing an Event, changing your Page settings or writing on a Wall — even your own Wall. You can even add your company's RSS news feed, any feeds from a blog that you might have, or a feed of items from a feed reader you share that covers your industry.

You can choose from two types of features that post content to your Wall: the update feature and the Notes feature. When and how you use them is entirely up to you, so we discuss the uses of each one in more detail.

Updating your status

Using the update feature can be done easily by entering a status update in the What's On Your Mind? feature and clicking the blue Share button. This feature is limited to 160 characters including spaces (which is about 2½ to 3 lines of text), just slightly longer than a Twitter post. Be sure to click the blue Share button to post it to your Wall.

You may also add a link to an article or news item of interest for your fans. Always stay on brand; that is, the content should relate to your business in some way. And consider keeping it on the positive side. No need to associate negative news with your business.

To enter a Web site address into the What's on Your Mind? box, simply click the Attach link and cut and paste the URL of the Web page into the What's On Your Mind? box. That's the best part about using one-liners — they're short and unintrusive so that you can read them quickly and easily. (See Figure 6-1.)

Figure 6-1:
Updating
status
feature
including a
Link.

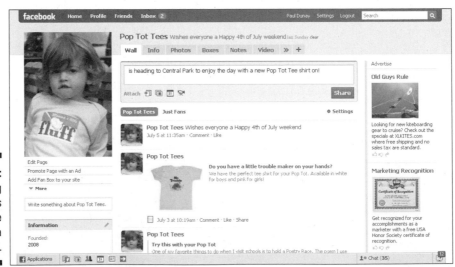

Using Notes for your message

The previous feature was geared toward a short burst of information. But what if you want to share a more complete story including a photo and tags? You use the Facebook Notes feature found by choosing Applications⇨Notes in the bottom navigation bar.

Of all the content-creation tools that you can use to share a post, Facebook Notes offers you the most flexibility. Notes are a good way to go because they have a title and body copy much like an e-mail or blog post and can be of unlimited length. Just watch the title though because you're limited to 120 characters including spaces although you should be able to manage that.

Notes can also include photos in JPG, GIF, or PNG formats with a maximum width of 396 pixels and a height up to three times the width. Maximum file size is 4MB.

In this example, we use Notes to announce an addition to the Pop Tot Tees line just in time for spring. (See Figure 6-2.)

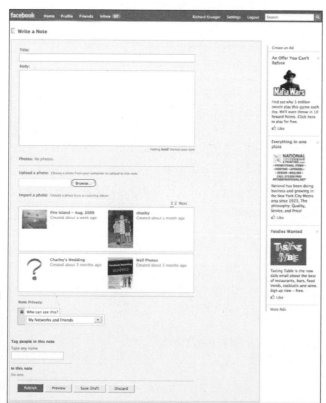

Figure 6-2:
Write a note announcing a new tee shirt for spring.

To add a note:

1. **Choose Applications⇨Notes from the bottom navigation bar.**

2. **Click the Write a New Note button.**

   The Write a Note page appears. Here you can

   • Add a title of up to 120 characters in length.

   • Type as much body text as you like, augmented with HTML commands.

   • Import a photo, or use one from your photo albums.

   • Tag someone in the photo to ensure he or she sees the Note.

3. **When you finish, you can preview your work and then publish your Note by clicking the Publish button.**

Fans can subscribe to your Notes much as they would to a blog.

You can use many popular HTML commands to dress up your Note.

Using Notes to import a blog

You can also use Notes to import posts from an external blog so that they appear along with your Notes. Facebook automatically updates your Notes whenever you write in your blog.

To import your blog using the Notes tab:

1. **Choose Applications⇨Notes from the bottom navigation bar.**

2. **Click the Import a Blog link on the right-hand side.**

3. **Enter an RSS or Atom feed address.**

4. **Check the box to represent that you have the rights to use or reproduce this content on Facebook and that the content is not obscene or illegal.**

5. **Click the Start Importing button.**

   You see a preview of some of your blog posts.

6. **Assuming you like what you see, click the Confirm Import button.**

   Imported blog posts cannot be edited.

If you import too many blog posts in a day, you could be blocked from writing or importing new Notes, which could result in your account being disabled.

Adding photos

Facebook also allows you to upload an unlimited number of photos and albums to your Facebook Page. You can reorder photos, rotate them, and acknowledge a Facebook member by "tagging" them in the photo. We explain how to tag a photo later in this chapter in the "Checking Out Seven Free Ways To Market Your Page with Facebook" section.

Adding photos is easy, and you have several ways to do so. You can post a single photo, add a photo to an existing album, or take a photo if you have a camera attached to your computer.

To add photos, choose Applications⇨Photos from the bottom navigation bar. Then, click the Create a Photo Album button. You need to name your album, add a location, and then provide a short description. Next, browse your hard drive or insert a CD-ROM to find the photo you want (see Figure 6-3), click the green check box in the upper left-hand corner of the photo, and then click Upload to post the photo to your Wall.

As with the Notes feature, you can also access Photos from the Applications menu, as opposed to the Photos tab of your business Page. However, you'll be adding photos to your personal profile rather than your Facebook Page if you post a Photo via the Applications menu path.

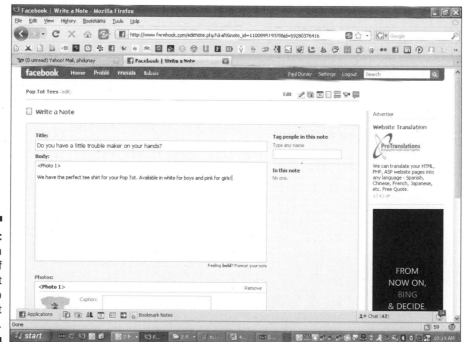

Figure 6-3:
Adding a photo of the newest addition to the Pop Tot Tees line.

In this example, we decided to promote a new product item for Pop Tot Tees by adding a photo. The photo really stands out on the Wall and looks engaging to the reader. (See Figure 6-4.)

Finally, you can take a photo with a camera if you have one attached to your computer. An Apple Mac has a built-in camera you can use to take facial shots or extend to take shots of live scenes. Give this a try if you think this will work well for your business. Be advised that you need to grant access to Facebook to allow them to use your internal camera, which you'll see is part of the process for taking a photo in Facebook.

Use images and photos that communicate who you are, provide what your business is about, and inject personality into your Page. Be sure these are photos you would want a potential customer to see — not the holiday party where everyone had a few too many cocktails!

Adding videos

Adding a video is just as easy as adding a photo. You have two ways to do so — uploading a video or recording a video. The easier option is uploading a video.

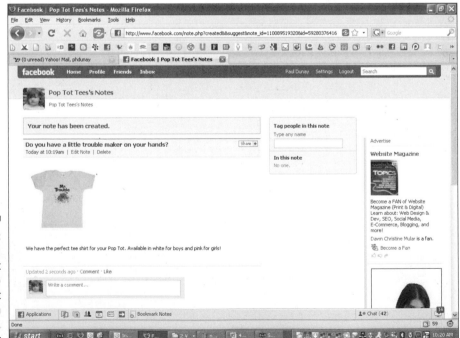

Figure 6-4:
Viewing the newest addition to the Pop Tot Tees line in our Wall.

You can add a video to your Wall by uploading one from your hard drive, a CD, or other storage device. All video must be under 1,024MB and must be under 20 minutes. You also need to agree to the Facebook Terms of Service, which stipulates that you or your friends made the videos you place on Facebook.

Recording a video requires that you have a webcam attached to your computer. Again, Apple's Mac makes this quite easy with a built-in webcam. But don't despair if you don't have a Mac, you can add a webcam to your PC with a FireWire or USB type of connection just as easily.

Facebook supports many popular video formats but does not support iframes or JavaScript.

To add a video:

1. **Choose Applications⇨Video from the bottom navigation bar.**

   The Video page appears.

2. **Click either the Upload or the Record button.**

   The Upload button asks you to browse your hard drive to find the video file you wish to upload.

   If you wish to record your own video, you need a camera integrated into your computer system with a good microphone. Also, you need to give Facebook access to your camera and microphone in the Privacy window that appears. Press the Record button again to begin filming.

3. **When you finish, you can click Play or Reset, which automatically rewinds to the start of the video.**

4. **Click the Share button.**

Adding a music player

If you are a band, a musician, or a comedy act, you may want to add the Music Player tab, which lets your fans listen to any MP3 tracks your company or band may have directly from your Page. (See Chapter 4 to learn how to add tabs and applications to your Page.) You can add as many tracks as you want because there is no limit. Keep in mind that the file size must be smaller than 15MB and the track cannot play automatically (it must be user initiated).

Facebook allows you to display a maximum of six tabs.

To use the music player:

1. **Click the Music Player tab.**

2. **Click the Add a Track link.**

3. **Browse your hard drive to find the track you want.**

4. **Certify that you have the right to distribute the file and that it does not violate the Facebook Terms of Service.**

    When the upload completes, you're asked for the song's title, artist, and album.

Your music cannot be played until you verify your Page. You need to establish that you are authorized to post the audio assets to the Page by uploading a valid form of legal identification, such as a passport, photo driver's license, or school ID. Doing so identifies you as the company's admin for the Page. You can upload a JPG, GIF, or PNG file of any of these identifications.

By submitting your identification, you represent that you will only upload songs or other assets to which you own the rights, and for which you have obtained all necessary music licenses. (See Figure 6-5.)

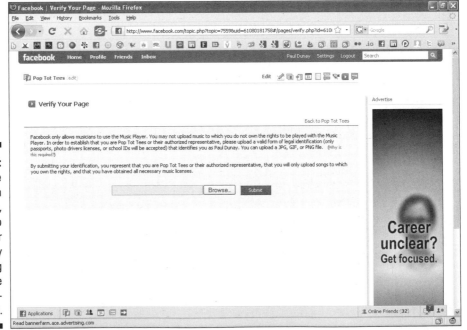

Figure 6-5:
To place music on your Page, you need to verify your Page by providing some identification.

Starting a discussion

Starting a discussion on your Facebook Wall is a great way to engage your audience. We suggest keeping it short and to the point. Be provocative in your title and give some content to help explain your position, and then watch what happens. Be sure to monitor the conversation at least daily and respond to as many, if not all, comments if you can.

A discussion is broken into two parts: the Topic and the Post. The Topic is limited to 120 characters including spaces, and the Post is limited only to your imagination from a size perspective. Unlike the Note feature, which is similar in look to the Discuss feature, you can't add a photo. For more about Notes, see the "Checking Out Seven Free Ways to Market Your Page with Facebook" section, later in this chapter.

To start your discussion, select the Discussions tab. If you don't see the Discussions tab, select the + tab to get Discussions from the list. Click the Start a New Topic button to begin.

Hosting an event

Facebook Events allows you to organize events or gatherings with your fans. It also allows you to alert your community about any upcoming events you may be having.

Generally, we think it is advisable for Pages to list any event you would normally post to your business Web site. If it is good enough for your corporate Web site, why not post it to Facebook? An event can be a grand opening, a storewide sale, an upcoming promotion, or a big industry conference you'll have a booth at. (See Chapter 8 for more information on hosting a Facebook Event.)

Sharing Your Page

The Share button, found at the bottom of the left column on any Page, lets you invite Facebook friends, or a list of Facebook friends, to check out your Page. Additionally, you can input an e-mail address of someone who may not be on Facebook so that they can view your Page.

To access your Page:

1. **Choose Applications⇨Ads and Pages in your bottom navigation bar.**
2. **Click the Pages link on the top navigation bar.**
3. **Access your Page by clicking the photo or the Edit Page link.**

Sending a Page to your friends

1. **Click the Ads and Pages link in the Applications menu in the bottom-left corner of the navigation bar.**
2. **Click the Pages link on the top navigation bar and select the Page that you want to share.**
3. **Click the Share button.**

    The Share dialog box appears, as shown in Figure 6-6.

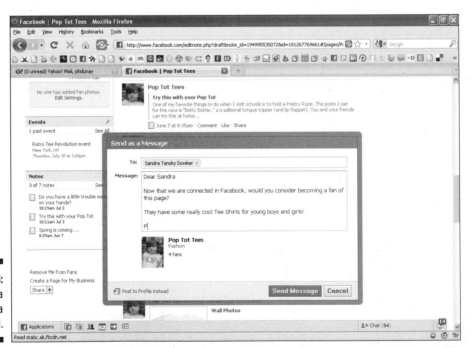

Figure 6-6:
Sharing a
Page with a
friend.

4. **Click the Send as a Message Instead link.**

5. **Start typing the name of a friend in the To field.**

   Facebook auto-populates the full name while you type.

   You can also type the name of a friend List, which Facebook also auto-populates, but be aware you can only message up to 20 people at one time so be sure your friend List is not too large.

   You can also enter the e-mail address of anyone you want to share your Page with.

6. **Enter your message in the Message field.**

   Because you are sending an invite to join a Facebook Page, be sure to mention the creation of a new Page or some reason you think the recipient should join you on this Page.

7. **Click Send.**

Any recipients who are not already Facebook members do need to join Facebook first to see your Page (see Chapter 2).

Posting a Page to your profile

The Share button, found at the bottom of the left column on any Page, also lets you post any Page (even if you haven't created them) to your personal profile to let all your Facebook friends know about it and how you feel about that Page by adding a personal message.

Here's how to post a Page to your profile (see Figure 6-7):

1. **Click the Share button found at the bottom of the Page that you want to share.**

2. **Click the Post to Profile tab.**

3. **Input a message about the Page.**

   It can be up to 787 characters in length.

4. **Click Send.**

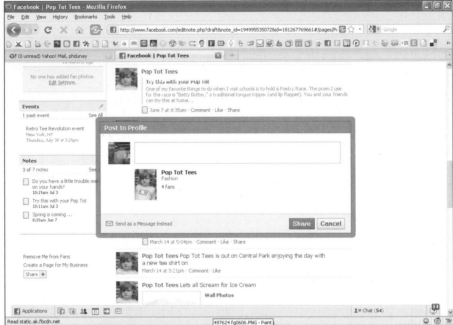

Figure 6-7:
Posting a
Page to your
profile.

Adjusting Your Page Settings

Now that your Page is live, your Facebook Page settings are actually important to consider. All Facebook Pages are public and therefore indexable by the search engines, such as Google. They actually do quite well achieving first-page search rankings under the name of the business, which creates even more of a viral effect for your Page. So, additional traffic can be directed to your Page from viewers outside of Facebook and you want to be sure that these visitors are respectful of your Page. You want to build a positive image for your brand and engage readers so that they engage with you and return often.

To adjust the settings on your Page, click the Settings link under the blue Share button on your Wall. (See Figure 6-8.) Page settings are organized in two distinct groups: View Settings and Fan Permissions.

Be sure that your Page is rich in the keywords that can best help you appear in the search engines. Also, be sure that you provide all the necessary contact information, such as directions to your offices, Web site address, and blog address. If someone who hasn't joined Facebook finds you through a search engine listing for your Facebook Page, make it easy for him to contact you without having to join Facebook first!

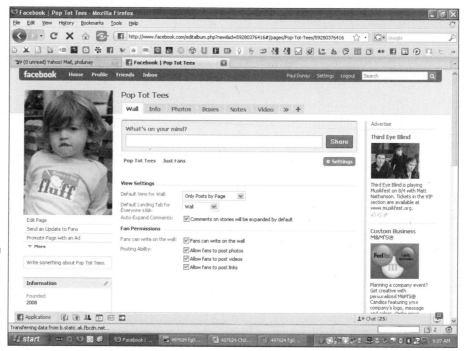

Figure 6-8:
Adjusting
the settings
of your
Page.

View settings

View settings control what users see when they perform certain actions. New viewers can be directed to a specific page and returning viewers can be directed to another page.

Default view for Wall

The default Wall setting here is Only Posts by Page. And we recommend leaving this as your default setting. Your viewers are greeted with what only you've written on your Wall rather than mixing it with what fans have written on your Wall. The Just Fans option underneath the What's On Your Mind? box lets you sort the results just for your fans.

The other option, Post by Page and Fans, gives you a different default view of both Page and fan updates, and two ways to sort: Just Page updates and Just Fan updates.

Default landing tab for everyone else

This setting allows you to direct new visitors to a variety of tabs, including Wall, Info, Photos, Discussions, and Boxes. This is the option where you can decide where you want your non-Facebook visitors to go when accessing your Page. But your fans can go directly to your Wall. For more discussion on tabs, see the "Using Tabs Wisely" section later in this chapter.

Depending on the nature of your business, you might want visitors to go directly to your Info tab to view your basic contact info. If you are an artist, you might want to send visitors directly to sample photos of your work. If you are a local landscaper, maybe you want visitors to see a video of your work. For Pop Tot Tees, we send visitors to our Wall to view our latest products and promotions.

Auto-expand comments

When comments are expanded, visitors can see the complete story for each post on your Wall so your visitors (both fans and non-fans) don't have to click to see more. We recommend keeping this option checked.

Fan permissions

Depending on the nature of your business or if your business is going through a rough patch, you may want to revisit these permissions. This section can help you restrict what fans can do and post to your site. Although we always recommend being as open and transparent as you can when using social media, there could be a time when you might want to restrict some of these settings.

Four options allow your fans to engage with your Page. By default, all options are selected.

Fans can write on the Wall

We think that you should leave this option checked. Unless you have a spammer or some other person taking liberties with your Wall that you don't think are appropriate, you can leave this setting alone.

Posting ability

These options allow fans to post photos, videos, and links to your Wall. Again, under the spirit of creating a conversation with your fan base, we think you should keep these boxes checked to allow your fans to post photos, videos, and links to your Wall and interact with you. Unchecking these settings seriously limits the interaction you have with your fans.

Leveraging Your Offline Customers

You are now ready to start promoting your Page to your existing customers to help build your Facebook fan community. The fun part about Facebook is that it lets you create a network that you can leverage when you have something to share. Sharing can be fun and, if you play it right, profitable for your business. Here's a look at how to leverage your existing customers to promote your Page.

Using your company e-mail

Because Pages have a unique URL, you can copy and paste the URL into your corporate e-mail inviting members of your database to sign up as a fan. This is a good way of going about it, if you really want to keep control of the branding surrounding the invite, which is definitely a positive. One negative consequence to keep in mind is that not everyone in your corporate database is a member of Facebook, which means, assuming that the recipient wants to become a fan, he needs to join Facebook first. This isn't all bad because it adds more people to the network — and everyone benefits from that. However, not everyone joins, so that's a potential negative.

Using the Facebook Share feature

If you want to use the Facebook invite process, you can do that, too. You have less control over how it looks from a brand perspective, but it is very consistent with all the other Facebook experiences your prospective fans are having. Here's how. Just use the same process discussed in the previous section, but this time copy and paste e-mail addresses from your corporate database into the To line and then include a message. (See Figure 6-9.)

Whichever way you choose to reach your customer, be sure you explain what value your fans can expect from you. If you plan a weekly thread on your discussion board, be sure to mention that and mention what topics you plan to cover — and follow through. If you are planning major events with big name speakers, drag them into the e-mail, too — mention any value you see your Page providing. In this example, I choose to use the pending spring launch of a tee shirt collection to entice them to sign up.

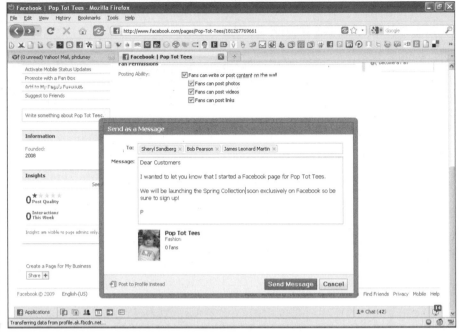

Figure 6-9:
Sending
invites to
your
customer
e-mail list.

Cross promoting your Page for extra coverage

Consider this scenario: you have a blog for your business, a Twitter feed, a new Page on Facebook, and oh yes, a Web site. You may think it is great that you are tapping into all these new forms of media, but how can you expect everyone to know about all these sites if you don't cross promote them?

Social media is a great thing, but the downside can mean fragmented media for many businesses. Therefore, a strong policy of cross promoting these sites is in order, and you have a variety of ways to accomplish this.

Be sure to cover the basics of letting everyone know about your various sites. You should include in your e-mail signature and every e-mail from your business all the ways that the recipient can connect with you. Also, be sure to list this info on your Web site Home page. For blogs, you can list your Page in a special Social Links section or with Facebook's latest plug-in called Fan Box, which can pull updates to your blog directly from your Page.

That's the cross promoting side of getting users to discover your various sites and pulling all of these sites into Facebook. Facebook provides a variety of applications that can plug in your blog feed, Twitter feed, FriendFeed, Delicious bookmarks, and RSS feeds to your Page.

Facebook also allows Facebook members to use Facebook Connect to connect on Web sites that have Facebook Connect installed. (Refer to Chapter 15 for more information on Facebook Connect.)

Checking Out Seven Free Ways to Market Your Page with Facebook

One of the great things about Facebook is that it provides you flexibility to engage with not only your friends but also your fans. In March 2009, Facebook relaunched Pages to be more like profiles. By doing so, this opened up Pages to the same types of interactions you use to grow your friend base.

We suggest you try some of these free ways to interact as part of your Facebook strategy. The only possible downside is that nothing happens, whereas the potential upside is you get some new fans.

Uploading photos or videos

A simple strategy for creating some interaction on your site is to provide content. Much like a Web site, you want to ensure you have a steady stream of good and engaging content on your Facebook Page as well. By uploading a photo or video, you reappear on the Walls of all your fans.

If you throw an event (see Chapter 8 for a complete discussion of Facebook Events) and shoot photos or video at the event, be sure to upload the media to Facebook and tag the people who attended. This is not only a great way of sharing the photos, but also a great way of appearing on the Walls of all their friends. This gives you immediate credibility with the friends of your fans.

Tagging for success

This great strategy directly links your Page to an individual Facebook user. The default setting for tagging in Notes or photos is that the user gets an e-mail letting her know she has been tagged.

When you *tag* (identify and label) the name of a friend in photos, videos, or Notes, the person who's tagged then receives an e-mail notification about it. Tagging, already a true attention-getting Facebook activity, is one of the most directly effective actions you can take.

To tag a friend or fan in a photo, follow these simple steps:

1. **Click the Tag This Photo link just below the photo.**

   The cursor turns into a plus sign (+).

2. **Click the face of the person you want to tag.**

   A pop-up menu displays a list of your friends.

3. **Select the name of the friend that's featured in the picture.**
   (See Figure 6-10.)

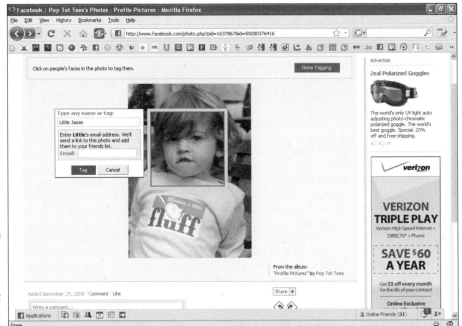

Tagging has some limitations, however. Facebook allows you to tag only people you know. For people you know (such as your friends) or current customers who are engaged with you (such as your fans), tagging is a helpful way to recognize them — just use photos or videos on your Page. Be sure to take as many photos as possible at in-person events (Chapter 8 tells you how to host your own event) and shoot as many videos as you can so that you can post and tag them accordingly.

If you're tagging members who aren't Facebook friends, you can enter their e-mail addresses to send them an e-mail notification and a link providing access to the image.

One way to obtain a suitable photo is to conduct a contest to find the best idea for your company or the best use of your product. Then take a photo of the winner with your CEO, and tag the winner in the photo in Facebook. (To find out how to host your own Facebook contest, see Chapter 13.)

When you tag a friend in a photo, that person is notified and the photo appears on her Wall. Your friend can delete the photo from her profile by clicking the Remove link next to her name.

The more people you can tag, the more your Page spreads.

Posting a note

Another way to appear free on your fans Walls is to post a note. You can either write a new note announcing some news about your business or repurpose a press release by posting it to Facebook.

To post a note, choose Applications➪Notes from the bottom navigation bar. Then, click the Write a New Note button on the top right of the page. Start by adding a provocative title and then post your text to the body of the note. Notes are reasonably flexible because you can format it with standard HTML commands and add photos to dress it up. Remember a note with a photo is read more than a note without a photo (see Figure 6-11).

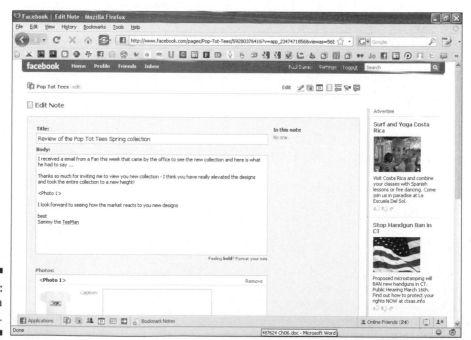

Figure 6-11: Adding a note.

Starting a discussion

Another great way to interact with your fans is to start a discussion on your Page. Keep in mind one potential benefit is that all discussions on Facebook Groups and Pages are public, meaning that they are entirely searchable by search engines such as Google. Oddly enough, however, they aren't searchable in the Facebook Search utility.

To start a discussion, click the Discussions tab. If you don't see the Discussions tab, click the + tab to select it from the list. When you reach the Discussions page, click the Start New Topic tab, as shown in Figure 6-12.

Commenting to win

Every comment that appears on your Wall, in discussions, or about photos, videos, and events is an opportunity to engage with a customer or potential prospect! Every time someone reaches out to engage with your Page, you should engage with that person in return.

Figure 6-12:
Starting a new discussion topic.

Failing to reciprocate can potentially backfire or cause less revenue. If you're asked a question, respond to it. If you receive a compliment, thank the person and reinforce your commitment to creating exceptional customer experiences. If you receive a mediocre comment, ask how you can improve the overall experience.

Using tabs wisely

Don't treat all your Facebook Page traffic the same way. One huge advantage that Facebook affords businesses versus a traditional business Web site is the targeting of new visitors on a specific tab of your Page. You can allow first-time visitors or people who aren't members of Facebook to navigate to one tab, such as the Info tab, and allow returning visitors to see another, such as your Wall.

By segmenting traffic and targeting new visitors with a special tab, you solve an age-old design problem that has existed since the start of the World Wide Web. This strategy makes sense because you don't want visitors to land on the Wall area of your Page and draw their own conclusions. You can control that experience by directing visitors to your most engaging information, such as a Flash video on its own tab or a well-crafted promotional offer on its own tab.

You can take this concept a step further by running ads on Facebook (see Chapter 9) and having them target specific tabs, or *landing pages,* in Web marketing speak) with different promotional offers on each one. You can then measure and monitor the tabs that work well and remove any underperforming ads and tabs. For basic information about the tabs feature, see Chapter 4.

Promoting your company blog

If you have a company blog, you definitely don't want all your hard work to go unnoticed on Facebook. Facebook lets you import your external blog as Notes on your Page to keep your fans and their friends up-to-date.

You are allowed to import posts from only one blog and the posts appear as a note on your Wall. Facebook automatically updates your Notes whenever you post a new blog post. However, be aware that imported blog posts cannot be edited.

If you have a company blog, be sure that you are synchronizing it with your Facebook Page so that when you post to your blog it automatically pulls the same content into your Facebook Page for your Facebook audience to read.

Chapter 7

Facing Facebook Groups

A great option for marketing your business on Facebook is Facebook Groups. In this chapter, we discuss how to find groups and join in on the discussion. We show you how to create your own group on a topic that can engage potential business clients, and how to promote the group to attract members and possible customers. Plus, we show you how to manage your group and measure its success.

With Facebook Groups, you can join and create up to 200 groups. Groups can be based around shared interests, activities, or anything you like. Groups are different from a Page (see Chapter 4) or a profile (see Chapter 2) since they are less about the business or person, and more about a shared interest or cause. Groups can be great, and perhaps a more personal option for marketing your business because you are relating to an audience around a cause or local issue that your business cares about so people can be more inclined to get involved.

What Are Facebook Groups?

You might have several reasons why you want to join a Facebook Group to help promote your business; conversely, you might even want to have your own Facebook Group instead of a Facebook Page for your business.

Groups are based around shared interests, activities, or anything you like. Pages are strictly for your business organizations, which includes artists and public figures. A good place to start is with a Page, but a more advanced marketing tactic may be to start, join, and be active in Groups that match your business in some way. (See Figure 7-1.)

Distinguishing Groups from Pages

For a Facebook Page, only an official representative of a business, public figure, nonprofit organization, artist, or public personality can create a Page and serve as its administrator (admin). Pages are designed to provide basic information about a business, featuring community building blocks, such as discussions and comments, upload user-generated content, and post reviews.

By contrast, any members can create a Facebook Group about any topic — and they do. Groups serve as a central hub for members to share opinions and discussions about that topic. Whereas Pages allow for a high degree of interaction and rich media with the addition of applications (apps), Facebook Groups do not allow for the addition of apps. (See Chapter 12.)

When an admin updates a Group's page, the News Feed story includes the name of the Group's admin. Pages, however, attribute updates to the Page and never reveal the admin's name. Groups also don't offer the status update capability, which has recently been added to Pages.

Figure 7-1:
A Facebook
Group
provides
members
with an
online hub
to share
opinions
about a
topic.

Group admins can send messages to the entire Group's individual Inboxes, provided the group has fewer than 5,000 members. Page admins, however, can't send messages to all fans. Group admins also have the ability to restrict member access by requiring a member approval process, whereas Pages can only restrict members from becoming a fan by age and location requirements.

The following are some key differences between Facebook Groups and Facebook Pages:

- ✔ Groups are not public, so the search engines cannot index them. Groups are only visible to Facebook members.

- ✔ As the owner of a Facebook Group, you can dictate how open you want your group's membership to be. You can make your group open to all Facebook members; closed, so that only Facebook members approved by the group's owner can see it; or secret, which is an invitation-only group that's not visible in a Facebook Groups search.

- ✔ You cannot add apps to a group like you can to a Page, so you are less able to take advantage of some of the more interactive features of a Facebook Page.

- ✔ Groups have it easier when it comes to recruiting other Facebook members. Unlike Pages, you can send invites quickly and easily to all your Facebook friends requesting they join your group.

- ✔ It's easy for your friends to send out an invite to all their friends to join your group — giving Groups a leg up on some viral marketing where Pages have a more difficult time.

- ✔ Sending a message to all group members is easier, and the message appears in the members' Inboxes. Inviting the group to an event is also easy (see Chapter 8 for more information on Facebook Events).

So you might want to consider a Facebook Group if you want to have a serious discussion where members can really get involved, perhaps around a cause or a topical media issue that you want to enlist support on.

The key is keeping the discussion flowing with the members of the group. You might be better off joining a few groups to see how it's done before jumping in to create your own. In the next section, we discuss how to find groups that might be relevant to your business.

Finding a Group

Finding a group is not very hard, and Facebook offers two ways to locate Groups: the Search feature in the top right of your screen or the Applications menu in the lower navigation bar.

Use the Facebook Search box

For our Pop Tot Tees example, we searched *tees,* but we also could have searched *T-shirts, kids,* or even *pop art* to yield some groups that we might want to monitor. The typical Facebook search for *tee shirts* brings results from all over Facebook. (See Figure 7-2.) Now, it's your turn.

1. **In the Search box, at the top right of your screen, type a name or title that interests you.**

   Be sure to select the Groups tab in the search results so that you are only looking at Groups.

2. **Click either the image or the name of the group that you want to visit.**

   In the search results, be sure to note the number of members, the type of group, and any recent activity, so that you have some indication of how active the group is before you visit.

You can also gain quick access to Groups by using the bookmark icon displayed in the lower navigation bar. Hover over the icons with your mouse to find the Groups icon, and click it for easy access to the Groups page. Remember that not all features display icons.

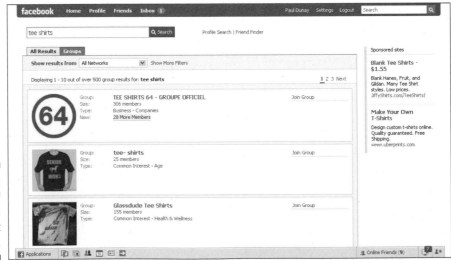

Figure 7-2:
Results of
a search
for tee shirt
groups.

Use the Facebook Applications menu

The other way to find Groups is to use the navigation bar at the bottom of any Facebook screen.

1. **Choose Applications⇨Groups.**

   The Groups page displays and is split into two sections. (See Figure 7-3.) The left side shows you groups recently joined by your friends, and the right side shows you groups you have joined.

2. **Click either the image or the name of the group to access the group's page.**

If you find a group that really matches with your business and you are thinking about reaching out to its members in an attempt to sponsor the Group, don't. It's a good thought, but that option no longer exists. Facebook did away with sponsored groups in favor of Pages.

When you access the Group's landing page, note at the top of the page any recent activity posted by the group admin in the Recent News section. Also, look for dates of any photos or videos that have been uploaded as well as any recent discussions on the Discussion Board. You might see how many members they have and whether you want to browse any related groups.

Figure 7-3: Finding a group that is right for you.

The most important part of the group is the Wall and the Discussion Board. This is really where the action is. But you need to join the group to get a sense of how active that group is and if you want to contribute.

Joining a Group

After you identify a group that matches your interest and has an activity level that matches with your objectives, it's easy to join the conversation.

All you need to do is navigate to the page of the group you wish to join and click the Join this Group link under the group's photo in the top right column. (See the preceding section on using the Search box and the Applications menu to find a group.) Keep in mind that you can join up to 200 groups and that each group appears under the Groups section on your profile. (See Figure 7-4.)

Participating in a Group

One of the Golden Rules of social networks and other forms of social media is to spend some time observing and listening to the conversation. It's good to get a feeling for the cadence or rhythm of the group's conversations before you barge in and change things.

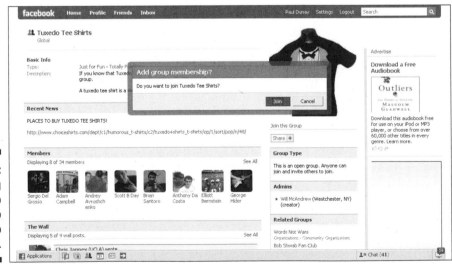

Figure 7-4:
Joining
a group
devoted to
the Tuxedo
Tee Shirt.

You'll find that only a portion of the group really participates actively and many members are just lurking in the background. That's okay, and don't let that discourage you from wanting to participate. If you are truly looking to learn more about Groups, then we encourage you to take the first step and jump into the conversation. It really is the best way to learn about how social networks operate.

You might also find that in some of the larger groups people tend to try to hijack the conversation by posting links to their own groups or related Web sites. Don't try this tactic. Technically, it's considered spam, and Facebook members have a very low tolerance for spammers.

Any member who is considered a spammer can and will have their profile shut down by Facebook. Although the rules on spamming are not published anywhere on the site, it is widely considered taboo by the members of the group, the group admin, and of course, to Facebook.

Creating a Facebook Group

When you get the hang of how a group works, as a marketer, you might want to start your own group to support your business. Creating a group is actually quite simple, and a group contains elements that are similar to those on a Facebook Page. (See Chapter 4.) To decide whether to create a Facebook Group or a Facebook Page (or both), see the earlier "What Are Facebook Groups" section to be sure a Facebook Group best matches your business objectives.

Securing your Group's name

Before jumping in and creating your group, we suggest that you conduct a search for the name of the group you want to start so you can see whether any existing groups or Pages have that same name. Having a name that has never been used on Facebook isn't required, but a unique name helps you to distinguish yourself, so we recommend it. Also, note that Facebook doesn't let you own a name in the same way as when you reserve a Web site address (URL). Other people can use a name that is similar to or even identical with other names on Facebook.

To conduct a search for group names, you can use the Search box at the top of any Facebook page, which we discuss in the preceding "Use the Facebook Search box" section.

Setting up your Group

After you choose a group name that you want to use, you can go ahead and create your group.

1. **Choose Applications⇨Groups from the lower navigation bar.**

   The Groups page displays and is split into two sections. (See Figure 7-5.) The left side shows you groups your friends recently joined and the right side shows you groups you have joined.

2. **Click the Create a New Group button at the top right of your screen.**

   Facebook displays the Create a Group page, as shown in Figure 7-6. In our Pop Tot Tees example, instead of creating a group based on the Pop Tot Tees corporate name, we created a group devoted to the best retro tee shirt fashions.

3. **Provide the following basic information about your group:**

   • Group Name: Because you did the research in the earlier section, "Securing your group's name," go ahead and plug in the name you chose.

   • Description: Be sure to put some extra effort into creating a good description of whatever your group is about. You want it to sound enticing to prospective members so that they will join. Usually, a statement that includes the benefits of belonging to your Group is a good place to start.

   • Group Type: Allows you to specify the type of group. Notice how the diversity of types here differs from Facebook Pages.

   Group types include Business, Common Interest, Entertainment and Arts, Geography, Internet and Technology, Just for Fun, Music, Organizations, Sports and Recreation, and Student Group. Additionally, many of the group types have subgroups.

   • Recent News: Consider this a bulletin board type of news. It could be anything, but again, be sure to pick something that people believe in and want to rally around.

   • Office: Either the name of your business or the name of the group.

   • Email: Use either a personal e-mail address or an address that you created just for receiving e-mail about the group.

   • Street: Street of your business location.

   • City/Town: City or town of your business location.

TIP

You do not have to fill in these last four fields — and in the case of city or street, it might be best to leave blank if you are seeking a national or international presence.

4. **Click the Create Group button when the information is just the way you like it.**

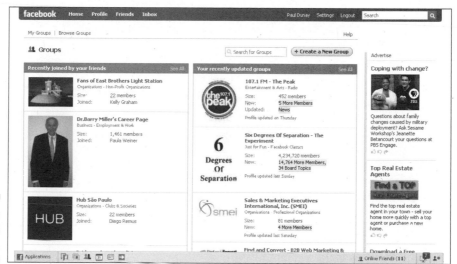

Figure 7-5:
The Groups page.

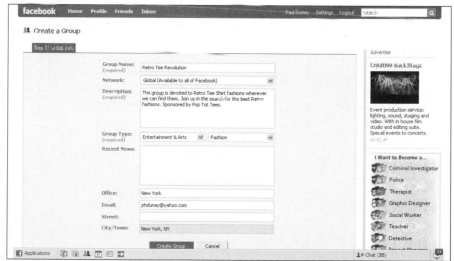

Figure 7-6:
The Create a Group page for Retro Tee Revolution!

Customizing your Group

After you create a Group, it's time to customize your group. You can now upload a picture for the Group; any picture that you have the rights to use and distribute in a JPG, GIF, or PNG format that is less than 4MB in size. (See Figure 7-7.)

You can also add a link to a Web site outside of Facebook or even to your Facebook Page, if that is appropriate, which links Facebook members to your organization.

Members of Facebook are generally more comfortable if you add links to locations within Facebook rather than outside Facebook.

The Options section (see Figure 7-8) is where you select whether it is okay for Facebook to list other related Facebook Groups within your Group and enable the Discussion Board, Wall, and Photos features.

These settings can help you restrict what members of your Group can do and post for other members to see. While we always recommend being as open and transparent as you can when using social media, there may be a time when you want to restrict access if a Group member is getting out of hand.

Figure 7-7:
Uploading a picture for your group.

You select the group's accessibility level in the Access section. The access levels of Facebook Groups are:

- ✔ **Open:** Groups that can be found by anyone on Facebook when doing a search. Anyone can join the group and anyone can see the Wall, Discussion Board, videos, and photos in the group.

- ✔ **Closed:** Groups that require approval by the group admin to join them. Anyone can see the basic group description information but only members can see the Wall, Discussion Board, videos, and photos in the group.

- ✔ **Secret:** Groups that can't be found by using a search or even in member profiles; they truly are secret. Membership is by invitation only; therefore, only members can see the Wall, Discussion Board, videos, and photos in the group.

After you are invited to a group or join a group on your own, you might spend some time observing the conversation before you choose to participate. To find out how to limit membership in your own group, go to the "Limiting membership" section, later in the chapter.

Generally, when setting access and publicizing the group, we recommend casting the widest net for your business. After you enter this information, click Save Changes to start promoting the group. Notice that Facebook asks you to invite your Friend List to join the group. You can pass on this for now until you read about promoting your group in the upcoming "Restricting Membership" section.

Figure 7-8:
Setting up the dynamics of your group.

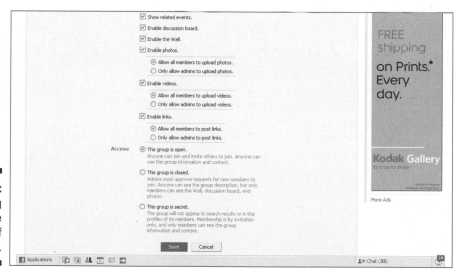

Promoting Your Facebook Group

After you create your Facebook Group, you need to promote the group and keep it updated with fresh content. Facebook Groups work similar to a blog or a forum in the sense that you can use them to communicate with a large audience quickly and easily. But building that audience is the real trick.

Growing your group is a never-ending process. Existing members need to see that new members are joining all the time to reinforce their confidence in the group — sort of a third-party validation. And the more members you have means the more people viewing your content and the more perspectives in your discussions.

A popular theory states that 90 percent of the participants in the group are silent, 9 percent are sometimes active, and 1 percent are very active. Therefore, if you have 200 or 300 members, only two – three people are very active, and one of them is you.

One method of building your membership in the group is to promote your group with an advertisement. You can use the Promote Group with an Ad link under the group's main photo with three simple and easy steps. (See Chapter 10 for a full discussion of advertising on Facebook).

We tend to think of groups and Pages as growing organically. But with groups, you build membership by leveraging existing members to bring in new group members, as well as by having a healthy and varied discussion on your group's relevant issues.

Reaching out to Group members

Reaching out to all your members is clearly one of the fun and easy parts about having a Facebook Group compared with having a Facebook Page (see Chapter 4).

1. **Choose Applications⇨Groups from the lower navigation bar.**

   The Groups page displays and is split into two sections. (Refer to Figure 7-4.) The left side shows groups your friends recently joined and the right side shows groups you run or have joined.

2. **Click either the image or the name of the group to access the individual group's page.**

   In the right column, under the group's main photo, you see a list of choices starting with Message All Members.

3. **Click the Message All Members link.**

   A page displays that looks very similar to an e-mail form.

   Only the admin of a group sees the Message All Members link under the group's photo. So if you are looking around on a group's page, you won't see this option.

4. **Write a short message on your hot topic in the Subject line and a deeper explanation in the Message area.**

   You can get the word out very quickly and keep your members engaged with the group. (See Figure 7-9.)

5. **Click send to message all the members.**

   Also, if you have more than 1,200 members, Facebook does not allow you to send a message to everyone, only groups of 1,200 or less have this option.

You might want to decide how often you want to reach out to your group's members. Your contact strategy can range from daily to monthly. In our opinion, daily might be too often for some organizations, but not if you're running a political campaign and your Facebook Group is the center of your community. Weekly might be okay for some businesses where special deals are offered that are available only on Facebook. We tend to think bi-monthly is a good cadence for most businesses and that monthly might not be enough to keep your members' interest piqued.

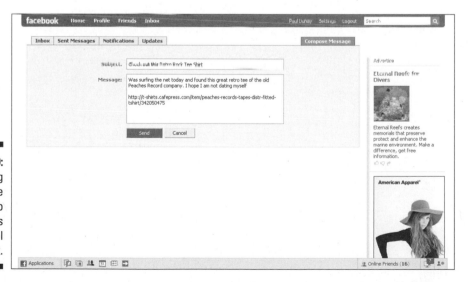

Figure 7-9:
Composing
a message
for all group
members
with a cool
link.

Anyone who joins your group after you send a message to your members does not know the message was sent.

If you want to invite people to respond to your message by commenting or joining the discussion, the Wall or the Discussion Board is your best bet.

Generating comments

Just like any good blog on the Web, members of your group come back repeatedly when the content stays fresh and is relevant to their needs. Therefore, you should try to provoke discussion by posting relevant links to external blog posts, research papers, case studies, online magazine articles, news sites, and so on. Besides links, consider uploading images and videos for your members to view — for example, if you're into travel, why not post pictures or videos of great looking destinations!

We find most of the comments happen on either the Wall or the Discussion Board. Generally, we find that the Wall is used for more casual comments, such as, "I totally agree!" or "Great idea." They don't further the discussion, but they do help by appearing on that members' News Feed and all their friends' News Feeds, giving your group more visibility and the chance that someone who is just a casual commenter might want to join your group. Think of them like a mini endorsement!

The Discussion Board is really where the debate happens. You should actively try to keep the conversation going on your group with a cadence of regular discussion topics. You might want to generate a list of weekly discussion topics that you can use to keep things moving forward. Having a strong discussion topics list allows you to always have an idea available. Alternatively, when new ideas come to mind or something happens in the media, you can use them to jumpstart a discussion.

Posting to your Discussion Board is quick and easy. If you are posting for the first time, you see a link on your Discussion Board that reads, "There are no discussions. Start the first topic." Select that link, type your topic and post, and click the Post New Topic button when you finish. (See Figure 7-10.)

If you have an initial discussion topic, then you can go to the Discussion Board and select the Start New Topic or See All links to continue.

A strong group has lots of discussions, and with any luck, provides some healthy debate about the issues. So don't be afraid to provoke a debate; that's what you're hoping to achieve!

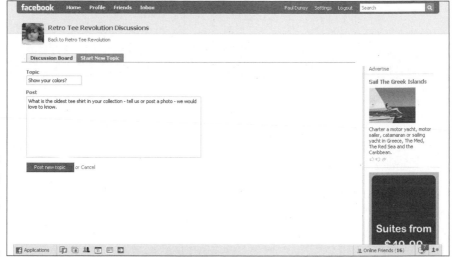

Figure 7-10:
Starting
a new
discussion
topic.

Managing Your Group

After you know how to promote your group and keep the discussion flowing, you might want to think more broadly about how to manage and measure your group.

Here are some metrics you can use to measure the success of your Facebook Group:

- ✔ Number of members in your group
- ✔ New members who join per day/week/month
- ✔ Ratio of new members to people who left the group
- ✔ Ratio of members who are Facebook friends versus non-friends
- ✔ Activity on Wall and Discussion Board
- ✔ Members who accept invitations to join your events

You don't have to use all of these metrics, although they are good indicators of how your group is performing. We suggest picking a few and monitoring them with either a spreadsheet or database so you have a way of understanding the trends in the data. Sure, you can see that membership has gone from 124 to 136 in one month, but what if you didn't know that is a 10 percent jump, down relative to last month's jump of 22 percent?

Limiting membership

Changing the group's type is easy. You can make your group open to all Facebook members; closed so that only Facebook members approved by the group's owner can see it; or secret, which is an invitation-only group that's not visible in a Facebook Groups search.

1. **Go to your Facebook Group.**

   In the right column under the group's main photo, you should see a list of links.

2. **Select the Edit Group link.**

3. **Select the Customize tab.**

4. **Select the Group Type that you want.**

5. **Click Save.**

Depending on your need or the development of your group, you might want the group closed until you're fully ready to launch.

Deleting a Group

Removing or deleting a Facebook Group is relatively easy. All you need to do is to remove all members from the group, remove the other group admin (if any), and then remove yourself. You see a message that reads, "You are attempting to remove yourself from a group for which you are the last member. If you remove yourself, the group will be deleted."

Facebook runs a periodic sweep of Groups aimed to remove empty groups. So Facebook takes care of deleting the group a short time after you empty it of the members and admin.

Chapter 8

Hosting Facebook Events

. . . .

. . . .

Facebook Events are a great way of getting people together virtually or in person to support your business, brand, or product. They are also an economical way of getting the word out beyond your normal in-house marketing list by inviting the fans of your Facebook Page (see Chapter 4) or the members of your Facebook Group (see Chapter 7). Fans can also help you promote your Facebook Event by sharing the event with a group of their friends when it seems of value.

You may want to RSVP to and attend an event to see how the process works. This should give you a feeling for how Facebook Events are done and what you may need for throwing your own event.

In this chapter, we cover how to find relevant events that you may want to attend and how to add events to your Page or group's Events list. We also discuss creating your event and promoting it to your fans, listing your event, and best practices for managing your event and following up afterward.

Getting Started with Facebook Events

If you have been a member of Facebook for a while, no doubt you have been invited to a Facebook event by now. They typically appear in your e-mail as an invite and a reminder on your Home page when you first log in to Facebook.

If you have never received an invite, don't despair. You can always find plenty of events to attend by choosing Applications⇨Events on the bottom navigation bar. (See Figure 8-1.)

After you have created an Event, you can also gain quick access to Events with the icon displayed in the lower navigation bar. Hover your mouse on the icon and click Events for easy access to the Events page. Remember that not all applications display an icon. Facebook displays six icons at a time.

After you select Events, Facebook displays the Events page, which tracks all present and future events. If you are new to Facebook, this area will be empty. (See Figure 8-2.)

Exploring the Events page

If you find a Facebook Event that you might want to attend, or share with your friends or on your Page, you can check it out first in the Event's preview page (see Figure 8-3). The Events page shows you the who, what, where, when, and why of several events without having to click through to the event's full page.

To view more details about an event, you can click the name of the event link or click the photo or title to open the Event page. (See Figure 8-4.) You may also want to view the guest list by clicking the View Guestlist link to see how popular the event is with your friends (who is presented first in the list) and non-friends (who is presented after).

Figure 8-1:
The Events option as listed in the Applications menu.

Events →

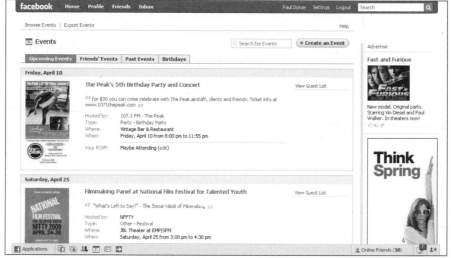

Figure 8-2:
Facebook
Events
manager
screen.

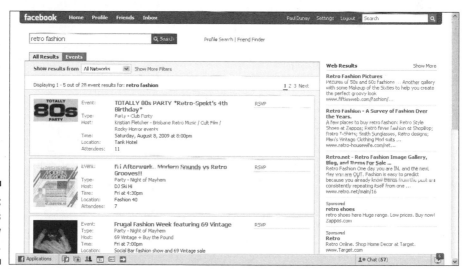

Figure 8-3:
The Events
preview
screen.

Each Event page has the following elements on the left column:

- **Name:** The name of the event.
- **Host:** The name of the host or organizing firm.
- **Type:** Facebook's pre-defined categories, such as Party, Causes, Education, Meetings, Music/Arts, Sports, Trips, Other, and so on. And Facebook's pre-defined subcategories, such as Business Meeting, Club/Group Meeting, Convention, Dorm/House Meeting, Informational Meeting, and so on.
- **Date:** The time the event starts.
- **Time:** The time the event ends.
- **Location:** Where the event will be held.
- **Street Address:** The event street address.
- **City/Town:** The event city or town.
- **Description:** Text used to describe the event.
- **Photos:** Photos uploaded about or after the event.
- **Videos:** Videos uploaded about or after the event.
- **The Wall:** Comments and Conversations about the event.

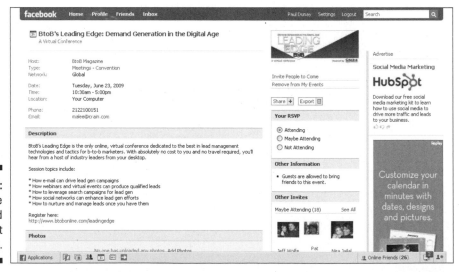

Figure 8-4:
View the detailed Event screen.

Each Event page has the following elements on the right column:

- ✔ **Photo:** A photo about the event.
- ✔ **Share:** Where you can post to your profile or send a message about the event to your friends.
- ✔ **Export:** The feature that allows you to export a calendar invite.
- ✔ **Your RSVP:** Where to change your status from Attending to Maybe Attending to Not Attending.
- ✔ **Other Information:** Information could include whether you can bring a guest with you.
- ✔ **Other Invitees:** The names and photos of those that are yet to be confirmed guests.
- ✔ **Event Type:** The information on whether the event is open, closed, or secret.
- ✔ **Admins:** The name(s) of the administrators of the event.

Every Facebook Event has its own page and URL, which makes it easy for you to invite nonmembers to your Event. Many of the details from the preview are carried over to the Event page, but you also see two of the most important Event features: the Wall for this Event and who's invited to this Event. (See Figure 8-5.)

Figure 8-5: Checking out who's coming to this event and any comments on the Wall.

Confirmed Guest lists are a good place to find new friends for your personal Facebook network.

In addition to the more complete description of the event, the Wall gives you an indication of the tenor of the conversation you can expect at the event. Also, looking at the Confirmed Guests section, as well as the RSVPs in the Other Invites section, gives you a better idea of who is coming and who you might be able to network with.

Finding an event

On Facebook there are plenty of Events happening everyday! And finding an Event that interests you is actually quite easy. You can find relevant events two ways: search for events using the Search box in the upper right of any Events page or look at your friend's events on the Friends' Events tab. We cover each using our Pop Tot Tees example.

Using the Events Search box

The Search box on the Events page is located next to the Create an Event button near the top right of your screen. You just need to plug in relevant keywords to get a result.

Don't expect the search to be as good as Google. It won't correct your spelling or suggest other events based on relevant keywords. If you don't find what you're looking for with your first search, search with alternative keywords.

Searching with the keyword *Retro Fashion,* we found the Oh So Retro event, which might be of interest to Pop Tot Tees fans or Retro Tee Revolution group members. Therefore, we might want to RSVP for this event in order to promote the event to our Page fans or Group members. (See Figure 8-6.)

Browsing the Friends' Events tab

If searching for an event doesn't turn up anything interesting, then looking at what events your Facebook friends are looking at is another option. As you know by now, Facebook is built to be social — so it's perfectly okay to look at what your friends may be doing. This is why we recommend building a strong social network to help you leverage its power when you need it.

Build your Facebook friends network before you need it — it comes in handy when looking for events or other more viral aspects of Facebook.

To locate events that your friends may be attending — select the Friends' Events tab on the Events page, which shows you any events your friends have added to their Events list. (See Figure 8-7.)

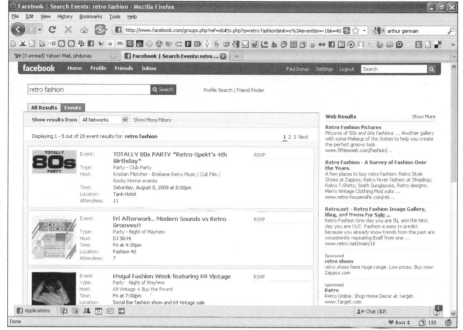

Figure 8-6:
Search
results
for the
keyword
*Retro
Fashion.*

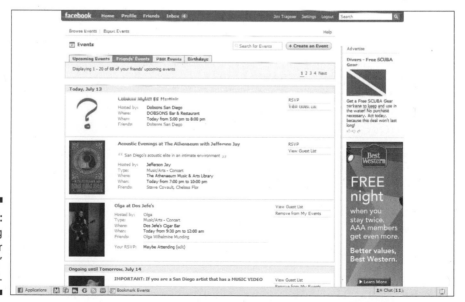

Figure 8-7:
Browsing
your
Friends'
Events list.

Adding an event to your Events list

Assuming you take the plunge and decide to attend an event, click the RSVP link next to the Event name. The event appears on your Wall and in your Events tab (see Chapter 4 to learn about the + tab) for everyone in your personal network to see. (See Figure 8-8.)

After you add an event, you see two new links on the Event page: Invite People to Come and + Share. What's great about Facebook is there's no shortage of ways for you to get the word out about an event you're attending to your network.

Using Invite People to Come

Selecting the Invite People to Come link takes you to the Invite Friends page. Here you can invite friends who are in your friend List. (See Figure 8-9.)

If you wish to share this event more directly with your friends or fans, then you can always click the + Share button located above the RSVP section on the Event details page.

You can also invite people who are not part of Facebook to this event by typing their e-mail addresses into the Invite Friends by E-mail box; separate the addresses by commas.

Inviting non-Facebook members to an event means they need to register with Facebook before responding to your request — so be judicious about the use of this option.

Figure 8-8: Events that you are attending show in your News Feed.

After you load the names of the people you wish to invite, all you need to do is add a personal message, and then click Send Invites.

Using the Share feature

Alternatively, you can use the + Share link to inform friends about an event. The Share feature is similar to an e-mail. You can invite individual friends by typing their names or invite entire Friend Lists up to 20 people at a time. (See Figure 8-10.) For more information on using the Share feature, see Chapter 6.

Figure 8-9:
Inviting people to an event.

Figure 8-10:
Sharing events with a list of friends.

Synchronizing Events with your Calendar

Every Event page has an Export link on it. With this link, you can quickly add the Facebook Event to your favorite scheduling program, such as Microsoft Outlook, Google Calendar, and Apple iCalendar.

Simply click the Export button located above the RSVP section on the right side of the Events page. Facebook offers you an iCalendar format which you can change and save as a different format if you need to.

Creating an Event

Facebook Events helps you with the fine points of creating and throwing your own event. Generally, we think Pages should list any event you would normally post to your business Web site. If it's good enough for your corporate Web site, post it to Facebook — but you need to know how to create an event.

After you've been through the process a time or two, you should be able to create a Facebook Event quickly and easily. If you want to throw an event for your Page, go to your Page to create the event.

To go to your Page:

1. **Choose Applications⇨Ads and Pages at the bottom-left corner of the navigation bar.**

2. **Click the Pages link at the top of your screen.**

3. **To go to your Page, either click the Photo or the Edit page link.**

Entering event info

Start by choosing Applications⇨Events from the lower navigation bar to go to the Events page. Click the Create an Event button in the upper-right corner to display the Event Info tab. (See Figure 8-11.)

You can add Events to your applications' bookmarks and drag them to reorder them. Facebook allows up to six applications in your applications toolbar.

To fill out the event's information, you need the following:

✔ **Title:** The name of the event.

✔ **Tagline:** The purpose or reason for the event.

✔ **Location:** Where the event will be held.

✔ **Start Time:** The time the event will start.

✔ **End Time:** The time the event will end.

✔ **Privacy:** Facebook allows you to restrict access to your Event depending on what your business goals might be.

  • *This Event Is Open:* Anyone can join the event and see the Wall, discussion board, videos, and photos on the event's page.

  • *This Event Is Closed:* Anyone can view the basic event information and then request an invitation for themselves, but only invitees on the guest list can see the Wall, discussion board, videos, and photos on the event's page.

  • *This Event Is Secret:* By definition, these events cannot be found by using Search or by browsing the profiles of the friends; the events truly are secret. These are invitation-only events; therefore, only the invitees can see the Wall, discussion board, videos, and photos on the event's page.

Figure 8-11:
Entering
the details
about our
event.

After you enter this information, click the Create Event button. The Customize tab appears.

Customizing event settings

Now is your chance to liven up your event's page with an image that can get some attention. If no image is chosen, a question mark displays.

With all images on Facebook, be sure you have the right to distribute the image because you'll be asked to certify this.

The Internet offers plenty of sources for royalty free images, such as iStock-Photo, so be sure to use one if you don't have a proprietary image from your business.

Photos come in many standard formats. However, you can only upload photos to Facebook in JPG, GIF, or PNG formats. Pictures can be 396 pixels wide with a height up to 3x the width. Maximum file size is 4MB.

1. **Click the Browse button to search your computer for a graphic file.**

2. **Select the picture that you want to use.**

3. **Select the box to certify that you have the right to distribute the picture and that it doesn't violate the Facebook Terms of Use.**

4. **Click the Upload Picture button.**

Assuming you like how the image looks, you can move on to the Event Options settings. (See Figure 8-12.)

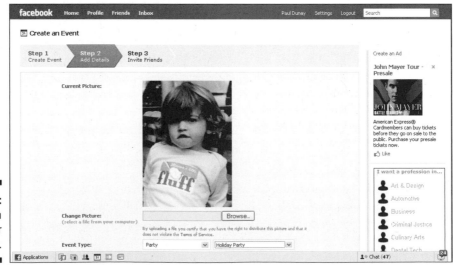

Figure 8-12:
Uploading a picture for your event.

Setting up your event

You can specify Facebook Event options, access, and publicity. You use these selections to customize your event quickly and easily. (See Figure 8-13.)

Event Type:	Party ▼	Holiday Party ▼
Description:		

Event Options:
☑ Enable the event wall
☑ Enable the event photos, videos, and links
☐ Only allow admins to post content to the event
☑ Allow guests to bring friends to the event
☑ Show the guest list
☐ Hide guests who are not attending

Save and Continue   **Skip and View Event**

◄ Back to Previous Step

Facebook © 2009   English (US)

About   Advertising   Developers   Careers   T

📘 Applications

The event's Options section lets you select the following:

- **Event Type:** Facebook's pre-defined categories, such as Party, Causes, Education, Meetings, Music/Arts, Sports, Trips, Other, and so on.

- **Subcategory:** Facebook's pre-defined subcategories, such as Business Meeting, Club/Group Meeting, Convention, Dorm/House Meeting, Informational Meeting, and so on.

- **Description:** A paragraph of text you can provide to describe the event.

- **Enable the Event Wall:** Allows guests to post comments about the event and interact with other guests.

A good use of the Wall for a Facebook Event is to collect questions for the event's speaker if one will be present.

✔ **Enable the Event Photos, Videos, and Links:** Select this option if you want to collect photos and videos of the event,m as well as links related to it. You can also select Only Allow Admins To Post Content To The Event, if you'd like.

✔ **Allow Guests To Bring Friends to the Event:** Enables the Invite Friends to Come feature, which we discuss in the earlier "Adding an event to your Events list" section.

✔ **Show the Guest List:** Allows the guest list to be seen. If you'd like, you can also select Hide Guests Who Are Not Attending.

When you complete this section, be sure to click Save. You can always skip Step 2 for now, but be advised you won't be able to go live until you finish this section. After your event settings have been customized, the fun now is to invite your friends to join this event!

Inviting Guests to your event

After you complete the Event Info and Customize tabs, you're almost ready to publish your event! Inviting friends or fans to the event isn't mandatory; you can simply publish your event and hope for the best. But Facebook makes inviting friends to your event so easy, it's hard not to.

After you click Save on the Customize tab, the Guest List tab appears. You can invite friends by selecting them directly from a list or by searching for friends with the Search box on top of the list. You can also invite an entire friend List you might have created (see Chapter 2 for a full discussion of creating a friend List). Best of all, you can even invite non-Facebook members to the event by typing their e-mail addresses (separated by commas) into the Invite box, or by importing their e-mail addresses from popular Web-based e-mail accounts, such as Hotmail, Yahoo!, and Gmail.

After you publish your event, it appears on both the Wall and the Events tab of your Page. You can also invite all of your fans by clicking the Update Fans of (your page name). They are sent an e-mail once you target the audience, and add a subject line and message.

Inviting non-Facebook members to an event means they need to register with Facebook before responding to your request — so be judicious about the use of this option.

After you fill in your list of invitees, you need to add a quick message to the invite. Provide something compelling for the reader, and make sure the value invitees can derive by coming to your event is front and center in your message. You can invite your first 100 people with this invite method. (See Figure 8-14.)

Facebook allows you to invite an unlimited number of attendees to an event in increments of 100, with no more than 300 outstanding invitations at a time.

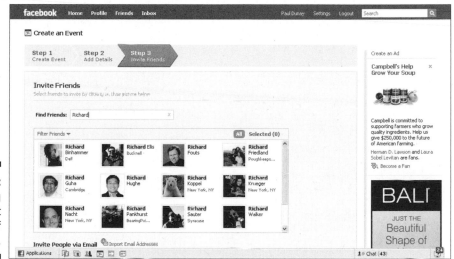

Figure 8-14: Sending out our first batch of invites.

Managing Your Event

After you set up a Facebook Event and send your invitations, you need to consider how to manage the event. Anything can happen at a live event, that is: Weather conditions can affect attendance, last minute speaker changes can alter the schedule, or an outright cancellation of the event can occur. These possibilities require you to develop a communication strategy regarding your invitees.

As you get closer to the event date, it is critical that you keep your event in the minds of your invitees. You might want to plan when you're going to reach out to them with a reminder. At a minimum, a good reminder protocol is to reach out the week before the event, the day before the event, and the day of the event.

Printing the Guest list for your event

Facebook makes it very easy to generate a printer friendly guest list for your event. You simply select Print Guest List, which is found above your RSVP section.

You can select which guest to print based on their RSVP, from those attending, maybe attending, no replies, and all attendees. It displays the names in alphabetical order and you can choose to add the person's profile picture to the print out by choosing the Show Profile Picture check box at the top. This can be enormously helpful in managing large events, where you don't personally know many of the attendees, or where event security is an issue.

Editing your event

Making changes to your event's page is easy. You simply click the Edit Event link found under the event's photo. You will be able to edit the Event Info and Customize tab you encountered when setting up the event.

Nearly everything can be changed about the event including the location. You can also notify everyone of any changes by posting a message on your Wall.

You can not change the name of the event once you have confirmed guests.

Following up after an event

Rarely do we see much follow-up after a Facebook Event, but we feel doing so is just good protocol. For traditional events, follow-up can be an e-mail, a phone call, or a written note, and we feel some of those techniques can apply here.

If you had a very healthy debate with lots of questions, you could post a transcript for attendees or even non-attendees. If some questions weren't answered because of time constraints, you could write the answers and send them to the attendees, too.

At the very least, a short thank you note to those that attended is just good form. As well, sending a 'Sorry you couldn't make it' note to those that didn't attend, perhaps with a recap, is also good form. Taking several photos of the event and posting them is the single best way to reach out. By aggressively taking photos, tagging them with the attendee's name(s), and posting them, you can leverage the power of the Facebook platform.

Part III

Strategies for Advertising Success

The 5th Wave   By Rich Tennant

"The top line represents our revenue, the middle line is our inventory, and the bottom line shows the rate of my hair loss over the same period."

In this part . . .

Part III discusses strategies that can help you advertise your products and services on Facebook. You can target your ads to a very specific audience and then create and test that ad to ensure its success. We explore the Facebook tools that help you optimize your advertising campaign and then obtain insights into your customers from their interactions with your Facebook Page.

We also show you how to sell your products and services on Facebook via the Facebook Marketplace, which can create a new source of revenue for your business and further promote your interests.

Chapter 9

Checking out Advertising Options and Strategies

*W*ith more than 200-million members worldwide, Facebook has the potential to reach an audience nearly twice the size of the Super Bowl's television viewing audience. The social network's ability to target down to the desired age, sex, location, relationship status, education, and interest marks a major paradigm shift in mass media advertising. It's now possible to reach a highly defined consumer market and pay only when one of those consumers clicks through an ad to the advertiser's Facebook page or other Web destination.

Facebook provides a self-service advertising model akin to Google's. Just like Google, Facebook allows you to easily create your ad, select your target audience, set your daily budget, and measure results. Ads can be purchased based on pay for impression (CPM) or pay for clicks (CPC). However, unlike Google, Facebook's engagement ads allow consumers to interact with ads in entirely new ways.

In this chapter, we show you how to use Facebook ads to your advantage. We introduce you to Facebook engagement ads: what they are and how to use them to fulfill your advertising goals. We offer tips on designing a link page to an internal Facebook location or an external Web site, writing ad copy (see Chapter 6), uploading an effective image, targeting your audience, and evaluating your advertising budget (see Chapter 5). Finally, we help you create your first Facebook ad and evaluate its effectiveness in fulfilling your marketing goals.

Getting Started with Facebook Advertising

The stakes are high for Facebook to have a winning advertising strategy. Advertising now represents the company's largest source of revenue and is expected to grow exponentially over the next five years. The self-service option is relatively new for Facebook and it's still lacking in many features that we surmise will come in time. The Facebook advertising platform shows tremendous potential and true innovation for both large and small advertisers. Figure 9-1 shows Facebook's advertising launch pad from which you can create a new ad or manage an existing ad campaign.

Facebook offers you an opportunity to form a sustained relationship with potential customers. By linking to internal Facebook Pages, you can keep the user contained within the Facebook environment. Just as you would approach any marketing initiative, it's best to follow your own pre-determined marketing strategy (see Chapter 5) when advertising on Facebook.

Figure 9-1:
The
Facebook
Advertising
launch pad.

Setting your Facebook advertising goals

In setting your goals for a particular ad or overall campaign, it's always best to keep it simple. Stick to one primary objective. Facebook users are on Facebook for social purposes. Keep your message to a single call-to-action. Make it simple, fast, and suited to the social nature of Facebook.

Facebook offers an incredibly *sticky* site for advertisers, meaning that users come back often. In fact, with a 50 percent daily return rate, consumers spend more time on Facebook's Home page than they do on Yahoo's, MSN's, and MySpace's combined.

You can place three types of ads directly through Facebook. This includes a traditional text ad, a display ad, which includes text and an image, and the unique Facebook engagement ads, which need to be ordered via a Facebook advertising sales rep.

In developing your overall Facebook advertising strategy, keep in mind the bigger picture. Provide a compelling experience for members after they click through the ad. Keep it social, because that's why they're on Facebook. Create an incentive for users to take the first step toward engagement.

Getting to know engagement ads

An *engagement ad* allows you to interact directly with the ad unit. Engagement ads allow users to RSVP to an event, become a fan of a Page, or watch a video, all without leaving the ad unit. For marketers who have a very specific goal (for example, drive more fans to the Page), engagement ads have the potential to drive a much higher conversion rate (see Figure 9-2).

Exploring a Facebook Ad

Facebook offers advertisers a number of unique ways to interact with Facebook members. From becoming a fan of a company's Page (see Chapter 4 to create your own) to confirming attendance at a Facebook business event (see Chapter 8) to installing an application (see Chapter 12), these actions are automatically turned into stories that appear in your friend's News Feed. Marketers who maximize these interactions by giving fans reasons to participate are transforming their fans into brand advocates, often without them even knowing it. (See Figure 9-3.)

Engagement ad

Figure 9-2:
A Facebook engagement ad allows users to become a fan without leaving the ad.

In this section, we prepare you for the placement of your first Facebook ad. We discuss setting up your ad link (*landing page*), writing your ad title and body copy, and adding your image. We also discuss targeting your audience and setting your advertising budget (see also Chapter 5).

Setting up your ad link page

If you are familiar with interactive marketing, you understand the importance of making a good first impression with your ad link. Your *landing page* (as it is known in advertising) is that page associated with your ad that the user views after clicking the ad and can be an internal Facebook page or external Web site. All engagement begins on the landing page. Successful landing pages provide an easy path to *conversion* — or realizing your goal. A conversion can include capturing data on a user via an input form, driving membership for your Page, or simply making a sale. Regardless of your objective, if your landing page doesn't deliver a desired result, your campaign is worthless.

Figure 9-3: A member's interactions with an advertiser appear in the headline of this sponsored ad within the News Feed.

Nowhere is the landing page more critical than when it originates via a Facebook ad. Facebook members are typically not in the habit of clicking ads. This is because they are on Facebook for social purposes, as opposed to browsing and discovery. Comparatively, Google's text-based ads generally yield a higher click-through rate because of the search-centric nature of the site.

Landing on a Facebook location

As a best practice, when running a Facebook ad campaign, link your ads to an internal Facebook location, as opposed to an external Web site. Facebook allows you to create ads that link to either an internal Facebook location or an external Web site (URL), but only one per ad.

For internal Facebook ads, you can link to a Facebook Page, application page, Group page, Event page, or Marketplace ad that you created or are the administrator of.

Furthermore, with the new Facebook tabbed format, you can link to specific tabs within your Facebook Page, delivering a more relevant Facebook ad that's optimized for your target audience. Conceivably, you can create a customized landing page within Facebook for each ad and audience segment. Figure 9-4 shows the Victoria's Secret PINK page — the company's landing page for a Facebook ad campaign — which is ranked sixth in most fans. It's easy to see from the figure why fans are so eager to engage with the landing page.

Figure 9-4:
The
Victoria's
Secret PINK
Page.

Everyone who sees your Facebook advertisement is a Facebook member. Don't take them away from the Facebook experience with your ad by leading them to an external page. Instead, bring visitors to your Facebook Page where they're just one click away from becoming a fan. Because you have access to your fans profiling data, your fan base can become an extremely valuable marketing asset.

Landing on a Web site page

Facebook also allows you to refer your ad visitors to an external Web address (URL), provided it adheres to the company's advertising policies and guidelines. If you choose an outside Web site, you aren't required to prove that you are the owner of the Web domain.

Advertisers might want to send visitors to an outside Web site for many reasons. Linking to an outside Web site offers advertisers greater control over their landing page's content, technology, and design. Advertisers might already have finely tuned landing pages that they prefer to drive ad traffic to, regardless of where the traffic originated. And, advertisers can employ much more sophisticated Web analytics on their site than is presently possible on Facebook.

Because ads can be purchased on a pay-per-click basis, you can opt to pay only when a user clicks through to your page, regardless of whether it's an internal Facebook page or an outside Web site. Figure 9-5 shows Party Poker's compelling graphics. The white-on-black color scheme and prominent usage of Facebook Connect (see Chapter 15) make this Web site for the company's Facebook application an effective landing page.

Figure 9-5:
The Party
Poker
landing
page.

Writing your ad message

Facebook is about making connections. Ad copy should reflect this spirit and maintain a familiar, conversational tone. With a friendly attitude in your headline and body, social stories generated around your ad have a more natural flow within the Home page News Feed. Given a 25-character limit on the title and a 135-character limit on the body, you can't waste a whole lot of words. Be direct, be straightforward, and be honest with your objective. Facebook is also about building trust, and your copy must show an openness and willingness to share and connect with your audience.

Facebook ads should entertain if the subject calls for it. Ads with a humorous message deliver higher rates of user engagement.

Choosing an image

Ads accompanied by images overwhelmingly perform better than text-only ads. Therefore, we strongly recommend that you include an image in your Facebook ad. If you use a photo, include a high quality picture with the maximum allowed size of 110 pixels wide by 80 pixels tall with an aspect ratio of 4:3 or 16:9. Image files cannot exceed 5MB.

Preferably, use images that are easily recognizable, not too intricate in detail, and feature bright colors without the use of the dark blue so strongly identified with the Facebook logo and navigational color scheme.

Targeting your audience

Facebook has made it very easy to target your desired audience. In fact, selecting your target audience is central to the Facebook self-serve platform. You can target by location, age, relationship status, and interests. You can even target by language, as Facebook Is available in 40 languages with many more in development.

Targeting your audience is as important as the message itself. Develop personas to represent your target audience. Learn what they're interested in — their educational background, relationship status, and where they live. Reach only the audience you desire by targeting to meet your specific business's ideal customer profile. (See Chapter 5.)

Facebook has focused its advertising strategy around its vast member data, allowing advertisers to target an audience segment precisely. You can say that Google's AdSense is more a question of where your ad is seen, while Facebook is all about who sees your ad. In fact, Facebook offers advertisers the ability to reach their exact audience — from a broad demographic, to a geographic preference, and to a more granular interest.

Facebook advertising is not directly *contextual,* meaning ads don't necessarily correlate to the content being displayed. An advertiser can't pinpoint where on the site their ads should appear. Google's AdSense, on the other hand, is a contextual-based advertising platform. Google's text-based ads are tied directly into the keywords being queried.

Targeting by location

Facebook allows for precise location targeting, based in part on your profile data and the IP address of the computer you log in with. Most cities in the U.S., Canada, and the U.K. allow you to add surrounding areas of 10, 25, and 50 miles for advertisers looking to reach specific regional markets, as shown in Figure 9-6.

Targeting by keywords

Facebook leverages its members' profile data to allow advertisers to drill down to specific keywords. These keywords represent a member's interests. Topics that users are passionate of, such as their musical tastes, television preferences, religious views, and other valuable psychographic data (see Chapter 5), can be used to further micro-target your audience. Never before has there been a mass medium that allows for this kind of precise targeting. By adding keywords to your targeting, you can reach consumers based on the interests listed on their profile page.

By micro-targeting, you're limiting the total reach of your campaign. By casting a wide net, you might be reaching outside of your target audience.

Figure 9-6:
Facebook
allows you
to target
by city.

2. Targeting

Location:	United States ✕
	○ Everywhere
	○ By State/Province
	⊙ By City
	Houston, TX ✕ Dallas, TX ✕
	☑ Include cities within 10 ▼ miles.
Age:	18 ▼ - Any ▼
Sex:	☑ Male ☐ Female
Keywords:	Enter a keyword
Education:	⊙ All
	○ College Grad
	○ In College
	○ In High School
Workplaces:	Enter a company, organization or other workplace
Relationship:	☐ Single ☐ In a Relationship ☐ Engaged ☐ Married
Interested In:	☐ Men ☐ Women
Languages:	English (US) ✕ Spanish ✕
Estimate:	569,100 people

Targeting
By default, Facebook targets all users 18 and older in the default location. You can change any targeting specifications you wish.

Location
Facebook Ads uses IP address and a user's profile information to determine a user's location.

Keywords
Keywords are based on information users list in their Facebook profiles, such as Activities, Favorite Books, TV Shows, Movies, etc.

More Help
Ad Targeting FAQ

Money, money, money — setting a budget

After you create your ad and identify your targeted audience, setting the budget is the final step before you can launch your advertisement. Facebook employs a bidding structure for its advertising inventory based on supply and demand. If there's greater demand to reach a specific demographic, the ad typically has higher bids. The company also provides a suggested bid based on the approximate range of what other ads reaching this demographic have historically cost.

Facebook's ads are based on a closed bidding system. You can't see what others pay for ads, nor can they see your bid. Facebook provides a recommended bidding range. As a strategy, setting your bid initially on the low side of the suggested range is a good idea. You can monitor your campaign to see whether the ad is performing at your given bid. Although Facebook allows you to bid as low as one cent, expecting a bid at that price to deliver any impressions is unrealistic.

You don't have to follow the Facebook pricing guidelines, but remember, if you bid too low, your ad won't appear.

Facebook also allows you to purchase ads based on a pay for clicks (CPC) or pay for thousand impressions (CPM). If your goal is to drive traffic to a specific page, paying based on CPC is probably the best performer for you. If your objective is to get as many people within your target demographic to see the ad, but not necessarily click thru, then ads based on a CPM basis could be your best option.

On Facebook, ads purchased on a CPC basis are more cost efficient at driving traffic to a given Web site or Facebook destination than ads purchased on a CPM basis. However, if your goal is more of a brand awareness campaign and you're trying to gain exposure to as many people as possible, ads purchased on a CPM basis could be a more effective strategy.

Putting your ad to the test

The social network offers marketers a full range of metrics to measure success, both from the Web site's internal ad management measurement or via Facebook's internal reports and measures. Because replicating an ad and creating different iterations for testing is easy, Facebook is quickly becoming the advertising platform of choice for savvy marketers. For a complete review of how to measure your ad's success, see Chapter 10.

Creating a Facebook Ad

Creating your ad in Facebook is quick and easy. Whether you're creating a text ad, display ad (text and image), or building in social actions, such as a fan request, getting your ad up and running in Facebook requires some basic steps:

1. **Scroll to the bottom of your screen, and click the Advertising link.**

2. **At the top of your screen, click the Ads Manager link to see the Facebook Ads page.**

3. **Click the Create an Ad button on the upper right of your screen.**

Design your ad

When it comes to designing your Facebook ad, it's best to keep it simple. Focus on one simple objective and be direct. Ads with images generally perform better than straight text ads. And, if your image features people, the chances are even greater that someone will click through (see Figure 9-7). For more information on designing your ad, see the "Exploring a Facebook Ad" section earlier in this chapter.

1. **Under Destination URL, click the I Want to Advertise Something I Have on Facebook link.**

   A list of your Facebook Pages, Events, and/or Groups that you manage appears depending on what you've designated for your business.

2. **Select the appropriate internal destination.**

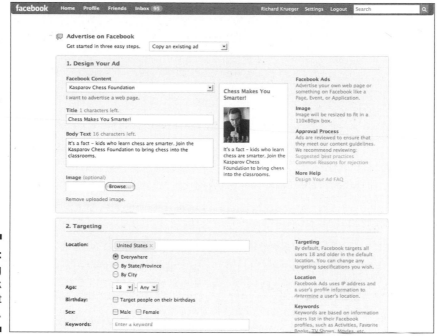

Figure 9-7:
Designing
a Facebook
ad is fast
and easy.

3. **Type a title, or headline for your ad.**

   Note you only have 25 characters and must adhere to the Facebook formatting policies.

4. **Add body copy with up to 135 characters.**

   Using all caps or title case caps is prohibited under Facebook ad guidelines.

5. **Upload an image.**

   Please note that this step is optional, but it is a proven fact that images do a better job at attracting attention than a text-based ad.

   Note also that as you start building your ad, you'll see it in near-real time on the right.

Target your ad

After designing your ad, you need to target your audience. You can think of targeting in terms of an archer's bull's eye. The closer you get to the center, the narrower the circles; the farther out you go, the wider the area. For more information on targeting your ad, see the "Exploring a Facebook Ad" section earlier in this chapter.

Following are steps to target your Facebook ad campaign:

1. **Select the location of the user you want your ad to be seen by.**

   There are nearly 100 countries from which to target and each ad can reach up to 25 countries. You can also drill down to the state/province or city level. For many cities, you can even specify between 10, 25, and 50 miles surrounding the city.

2. **Select the age range of the audience you want to see the ad.**

   You can use the default, Any, to reach the widest possible audience. Keep in mind, Facebook doesn't allow targeting to members younger than 13.

3. **Select Male, Female, or both.**

   You see Male and Female checked in the default mode, making the ad available to the widest amount of members possible.

4. **Type any keywords you want to specifically target.**

   Keywords are based on the information a user chooses to include in their Facebook profile. When you start typing a term, you see a range of possible words appear. You can click one of these words without completing your term. If the keyword you enter is not identified in enough Facebook members' profiles, it's not statistically large enough to target. You can enter as many keywords as are relevant.

5. **Select the desired education level of the audience.**

   You can reach high school, college, college graduate, or all.

6. **Target down to the workplace.**

   When you begin to enter the workplace, you see a range of workplace possibilities with those letters appear. If the workplace you're seeking to enter isn't statistically large enough to support an ad, it remains blank.

7. **Select the status of the audience's relationship.**

   You can choose between Single, In a Relationship, Engaged, and Married.

8. **Select which sex your target audience is interested in, Men or Women.**

9. **Type the target audience's language preference.**

   There are 40 languages listed and nearly 100 countries, and growing. Facebook offers a truly global campaign from one centralized management platform (see Figure 9-8).

   Note: As you narrow your audience, you'll see a revised Estimate of the potential audience based on your selected criteria on the bottom of the Targeting section. The estimate also recaps the targeting attributes that you have selected.

   When using keywords of interest to target an ad campaign, it's always a good idea to include those keywords in the ad copy.

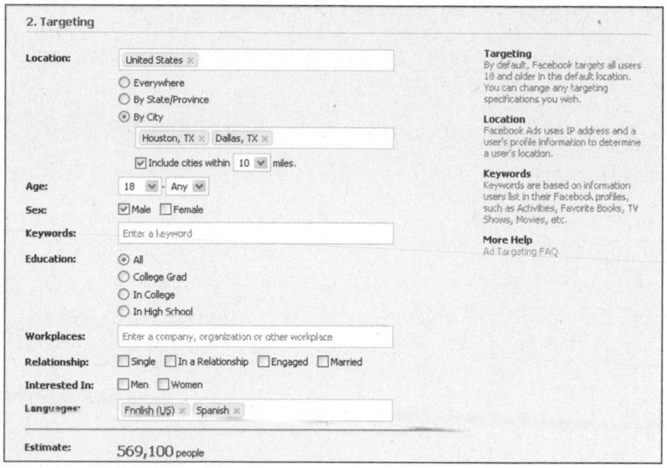

Figure 9-8:
Target your audience's primary language.

Campaigns and pricing

When it comes to setting your campaign budget, Facebook advertisers are wise to pay attention to their daily spend and performance results. It's always a good idea to get some benchmarks as to your campaign's performance. If you find you're click-thru-ratio (CTR%) is higher than 1 percent, you might consider lowering your bid, as a high performing ad gets preference over underperforming ones. The difference in a few cents can be significant, depending on your total spend, so you want to constantly adjust your bids to maximize your ROI. (See Figure 9-9.) For more information on setting a budget for your ad, see the "Exploring a Facebook Ad" section earlier in this chapter.

The following steps detail how to set your Facebook ad budget:

1. **If you've created a new campaign, type the name of the campaign.**

2. **Set your daily maximum budget.**

   Please note, the minimum daily spend amount is $1.00 USD, which means that you can run a Facebook ad for as little as $1.00 a day, albeit to a very small number of people.

3. **Choose when your ad runs, either continuously starting today, or within a specific date range.**

4. **Enter your bid.**

   Facebook allows you to either bid based on Pay for Impression (CPM) or Pay for Clicks (CPC). If you select Pay for Impression (CPM), remember you're bid represents every 1,000 impressions, or ad views. The minimum amount you are allowed to bid is one cent, although Facebook often rejects bids that are too low.

5. **Enter the maximum amount you are willing to pay.**

   Specify for either one thousand impressions, or per click, depending on your selection in Step 4.

6. **Click the blue Continue button at the bottom of the page.**

7. **Click the blue Place Order button near the bottom of the screen.**

   You are presented with a Review Ad page that recaps your creative, your targeting, type of bid (CPC or CPM), bid price, daily budget, and duration of ad flight (the time period an ad runs is also referred to as an ad flight).

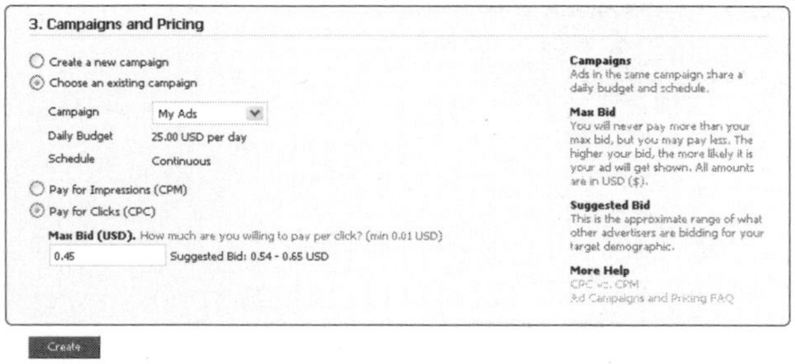

Figure 9-9:
Campaigns
and pricing
information.

Creating Multiple Campaigns

Facebook makes it easy for you to duplicate an existing ad, change a number of variables, and launch multiple multi-faceted ad campaigns. An advertiser has several reasons for doing this:

✔ For targeting many locations to tailor each ad to a specific region. Because economical, educational, and personal preferences vary from region to region, the ad copy and image may need to reflect these differences.

✔ To reach multi-language audiences, use Facebook's language targeting on an ad-by-ad basis.

✔ To test which variables in ads perform better to optimize the campaign to the better performing ads.

✔ To test different bids and models (CPC versus CPM) to determine which are more economically efficient.

The Ads Manager screen in Figure 9-10 displays all campaigns, both active and paused (campaigns placed on hold).

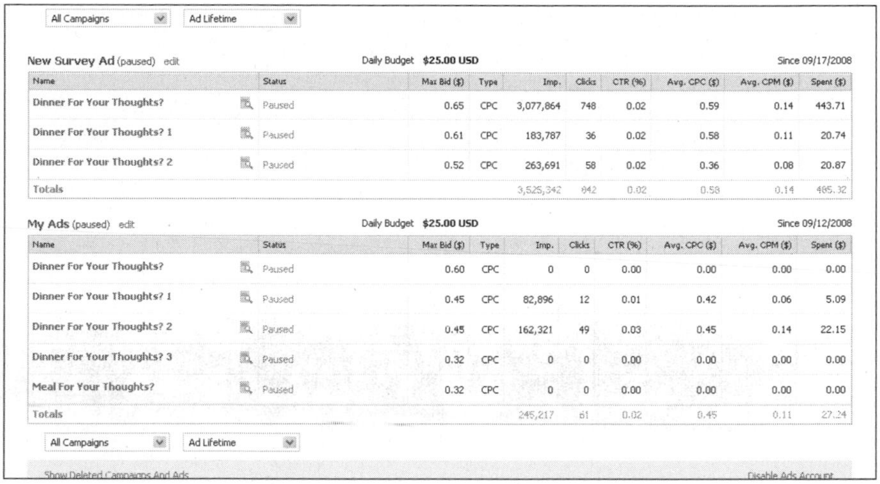

All Campaigns	Ad Lifetime									

New Survey Ad (paused) edit — Daily Budget **$25.00 USD** — Since 09/17/2008

Name	Status	Max Bid ($)	Type	Imp.	Clicks	CTR (%)	Avg. CPC ($)	Avg. CPM ($)	Spent ($)
Dinner For Your Thoughts?	Paused	0.65	CPC	3,077,864	748	0.02	0.59	0.14	443.71
Dinner For Your Thoughts? 1	Paused	0.61	CPC	183,787	36	0.02	0.58	0.11	20.74
Dinner For Your Thoughts? 2	Paused	0.52	CPC	263,691	58	0.02	0.36	0.08	20.87
Totals				3,525,342	842	0.02	0.53	0.14	485.32

My Ads (paused) edit — Daily Budget **$25.00 USD** — Since 09/12/2008

Name	Status	Max Bid ($)	Type	Imp.	Clicks	CTR (%)	Avg. CPC ($)	Avg. CPM ($)	Spent ($)
Dinner For Your Thoughts?	Paused	0.60	CPC	0	0	0.00	0.00	0.00	0.00
Dinner For Your Thoughts? 1	Paused	0.45	CPC	82,896	12	0.01	0.42	0.06	5.09
Dinner For Your Thoughts? 2	Paused	0.45	CPC	162,321	49	0.03	0.45	0.14	22.15
Dinner For Your Thoughts? 3	Paused	0.32	CPC	0	0	0.00	0.00	0.00	0.00
Meal For Your Thoughts?	Paused	0.32	CPC	0	0	0.00	0.00	0.00	0.00
Totals				245,217	61	0.02	0.45	0.11	27.24

All Campaigns	Ad Lifetime									

Show Deleted Campaigns And Ads — Disable Ads Account

Figure 9-10:
The Ads
Manager
displays all
your
campaigns.

Placing Ads through a Facebook Rep

Like all major media companies, Facebook has a staff of competent sales professionals at the ready to assist you with your campaigns. Purchasing ads directly through a Facebook representative has its advantages. A rep assigns you a campaign manager, who oversees all aspects of a campaign, from creating an ad to targeting through bidding, and optimizing your campaign. And, for those advertisers that can commit to spending a minimum of $10,000 per month over an initial three-month period, this is definitely a preferred option.

Although Facebook limits their handholding ad service to advertisers with a sizeable budget, there are significant advantages to this direction. First, advertisers can choose to have their ads displayed on the coveted Home page, where click-through rates tend to be higher.

Additionally, they're able to participate in Facebook's newest type of ad unit, engagement ads, which bring interactions with your brand directly into the ad unit. Examples of engagement ads include the ability to send virtual gifts, RSVP to an event, add a video comment, become a fan, or take a poll. Facebook's engagement ads are ideal for driving consumer engagement, collecting data, and raising brand awareness.

Facebook claims that their engagement ads have a higher action rate than the industry average click-through rate of 0.15 percent. They also offer extended reach by generating social stories around user's interactions with the ad, amplifying reach as they are seen on friend's News Feeds. If your budget is large enough and your objective is to generate engagement, engagement ads purchased via your Facebook ad rep are just the vehicle to meet your marketing needs.

To get in touch with Facebook's advertising staff, you can complete a contact form at `www.facebook.com/help/seeall.php?facebook&id=409#/help/contact.php?show_form=new_advertiser`.

Or, call Facebook's corporate headquarters in San Francisco, CA at (415) 467-2300 and request to speak with the advertising sales dept.

Ten Common Ad Mistakes

To maintain a high standard of content, Facebook places strict guidelines on advertisers. All ads require a review period, which can take up to 24 hours. Ads that are approved can be served immediately thereafter. Unapproved ads can be found on your Ad Manager page, under Status Unapproved. Ten common ad mistakes are

- ✔ Incorrect use of capital letters
- ✔ Incorrect grammar, spelling, and use of slang
- ✔ Inaccurate ad text
- ✔ Deceptive claims
- ✔ Inappropriate images
- ✔ Misguided targeting
- ✔ Improper sentence structure
- ✔ Use of language deemed inappropriate
- ✔ Incorrect usage of punctuation
- ✔ Symbols exchanged for words

Chapter 10

Measuring Advertising Success — One Click at a Time

In This Chapter

▶ Checking out your ad campaign mid-flight

▶ Evaluating Facebook reports

▶ Introducing the new Facebook Insights feature

▶ Measuring social engagement with your Page

*A*lthough in its infancy still, the Facebook advertising platform is performing well for thousands of advertisers. The platform's ability to target ad demographics is already legendary, and, because prices are determined by a supply and demand-based bidding system, now is probably the best time to jump in. Ads can be purchased on both a pay for thousand impressions (CPM) or pay for clicks (CPC) basis — at extremely low price points while supply far exceeds demand. Whether marketers are looking to micro-target their audience or reach as broad an audience as possible, there is no better social networking platform for advertising than Facebook.

Facebook offers marketers a full range of metrics to measure success via the Web site's internal ad management reports, exportable reports, and the new Facebook Insights dashboard, which lets you collect data on visitors to your Page.

We show you how to use the Facebook reporting tools to gauge the number of impressions, click rates, and other valuable traffic data, including number of fans added, demographics of responders, number of visitors to the Page, and those that engaged in an activity while on your Page (see the "Viewing Facebook Ad Reports" section later in this chapter).

And finally, we show you how the new Facebook Insight tools can provide you with the metrics to measure the effectiveness of your Page and maximize its potential (see the "Optimizing Your Page" section later in this chapter).

Testing Your Ad

As with all online advertising, it's a good idea to test several variations of your ad before you commit the bulk of your advertising budget. Facebook makes it easy to copy an existing ad, change the title, body copy, photo, targeting, CPM/CPC pay model, bid, referring page (internal or external), or any combination of the above (see Chapter 9 for details). Because you can set an individual budget for each campaign and track its effectiveness, you'll be able to identify the better performing ads. With some historical data, you can optimize your campaign by increasing the budget on better performing ads and decreasing or eliminating the poorer performing ones.

Test both CPC and CPM campaigns. A particular campaign with a strong call-to-action or offer is likely to have a strong response rate, regardless of its purchase model. If a campaign is targeting an extremely granular (narrow or highly targeted) audience, CPC-based ads often deliver a more cost-efficient ad buy.

Tracking your ad's success

The Facebook Ads reports, accessible via the Report link on the top of the Ad Manager page, allows you to keep a close eye on your campaign's progress. From the number of times your ad has been shown to the number of times people have clicked the ad and to the average cost of a click, Facebook offers plenty of data for marketers to track.

Today's savvy interactive advertisers live and die by performance metrics for a reason. They know that the best way to improve an ad's effectiveness is to understand the available data and make informed decisions.

Before you fully embrace or dismiss Facebook advertising, set some basic benchmarks to evaluate a campaign's success or failure.

It's important to note that on Facebook, ads purchased on a CPC basis are more cost efficient at driving traffic to a given Web site or Facebook destination than if purchased on a CPM basis. However, if your goal is more of a brand awareness campaign and you're trying to gain exposure to as many people as possible, ads purchased on a CPM basis could be a more effective strategy.

Testing your ad's link page

Smart marketers are continuously testing their ad's referral link (*landing pages*, as we discuss in Chapter 9), often employing advanced algorithms and tracking services, realizing that just a slight increase in the number of consumers who take on a specific desired action (often referred to as conversion rate), such as completing a form, has a dramatic effect on the campaign's overall return on investment (ROI). While not everyone has the size of budget that allows you to extensively test different iterations of a landing page, at the least, it's important to monitor your ad's performance, see what's working and what's not, and replicate your successes where possible.

Viewing Facebook Ad Reports

Facebook provides some basic metrics to help you measure your ad's performance. While the reporting engine is still somewhat limited, the site provides enough key data from which to gauge your campaign's success. These performance metrics also allow you to adapt or optimize your ad to maximize your return on investment (ROI).

You can view your ad performance from the Facebook Ads page by selecting the Report link on the top of the Ads Manager page. You can access the Facebook Ads page by choosing Applications↪Ads and Pages on the bottom left of your Facebook navigation bar. Just click the Ads Manager link at the top of your screen to be taken to the Facebook advertising start page.

Facebook personalizes information about your account's respective ads. The page features notifications regarding Facebook advertising at the top, followed by a grid detailing ad titles and their respective performance metrics.

A campaign view drop-down menu on the top left of the grid allows you to view by all campaigns, which shows multiple campaigns, each consisting of multiple ads; or view by ad title, which displays only the selected ad's respective performance metrics.

You can also select the period by which to view your metrics via the Time Summary drop-down menu. The default period is set to daily, but you can also select weekly (beginning on the most recent Sunday), monthly, or set the date range. Final "actual" stats may show slight differences from those reported during the ad's *flight* (the period during which an ad is shown).

At the bottom of the page, you can view your ad performance over time on a plot graph. A simple drop-down menu allows you to view by clicks, impressions, or click thru rate (CTR). This visual representation provides a quick-glance perspective on your ad's performance, indicating trends in the campaign, as opposed to a more granular by-the-numbers view. Figure 10-1 shows the Facebook Ads Manager providing all relevant ad data in an easy-to-view grid format. A graph presents key data visually across a timeline.

In addition to Reports, you'll also find tabbed links on the top of the Ads Manager to Pages, which provides centralized management over the Pages you administer and allows you to view each one's metrics:

- **Billing:** Change your billing information and view up-to-date balances
- **Settings:** Set up notifications regarding your ad's account
- **Help:** Takes you to the Facebook Ads Help Center

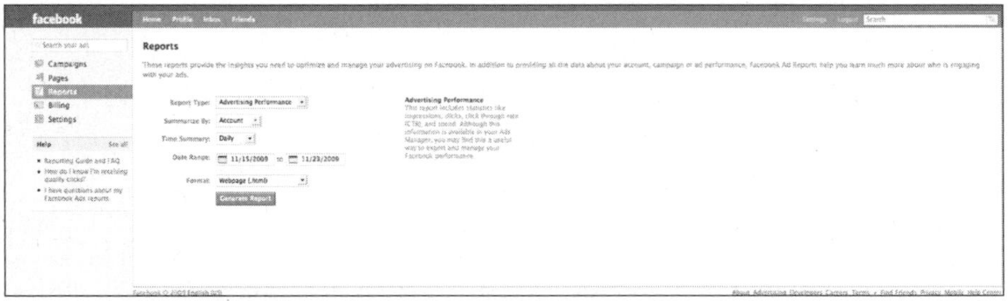

Figure 10-1:
Facebook
provides
relevant
reporting
data.

Measuring the frequency of the ad

Impressions, represented as *Imp.* in the shaded top row of the grid, indicates how many times your ad has been shown. If your ad bid is based on CPM, this key metric directly correlates to your budget.

Note that ads based on a CPC-type bid also benefit from a high number of impressions because it provides a valuable branding vehicle, regardless of the number of users that click thru.

Checking out the click-through ratio

The click-through ratio, shown as CTR (%) on the shaded row of the grid, shows the percentage of Facebook members who saw the ad divided by the number of members who clicked the ad and who were then redirected to the advertiser's page. This is a key stat for you to gauge your ad's effectiveness. A low-performing ratio of 0.01% means that for every 10,000 people, only one click per ad.

Viewing average cost-per-click

Next to CTR (%) on the grid is the average cost-per-click (CPC), shown as Avg. CPC ($), indicating the average price you paid for your ad. It's important to note that even if your bid type is based on cost-per-thousand ad views (CPM), it provides the average cost based on the cost-per-click model.

Optimizing Your Page

Facebook advertising is a learn-as-you-go experience. Fortunately, there are strategies you can use to measure the efficiency of your Page and maximize its performance. *Optimizing* means adapting, and it's very common to adjust your ads in mid-flight to lower your cost, increase your click-through rate, and improve your return on investment (ROI).

Getting a clue from Facebook Insights

Facebook also provides a set of performance metrics for your Pages, called Insights. These tools provide a dashboard view of key metrics involving your Page and how people are interacting with it. This includes reach (number of clicks), viral impact (number of fans), responder insights (demographic breakdown of fans), and levels of engagement (number of Wall posts, videos played, and so on). While it does not provide specific ad performance metrics (see above in this chapter), it gives you an idea as to who is clicking over to your Page and what they're doing once they get to your Page.

To view your Page's metrics, go to your Ads Manager page and click the Pages tab on the second-line menu bar. My Pages presents your Facebook Page(s). Click the View Insights link next to the Page with the data you want to view (see Figure 10-2).

Post Quality

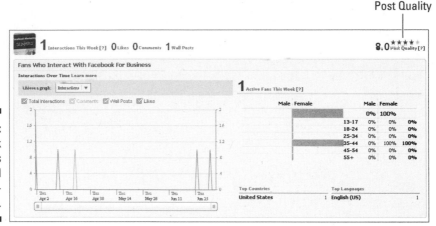

Figure 10-2:
Facebook
Insights
dashboard
provides in-
depth data.

If your Page doesn't generate enough activity, no measurements are provided by Insights.

Gauging fan interactions

The first measurement shows total fan interactions with the Page. Anytime a fan writes on your Wall, comments on a post, or indicates that they like the content, a fan interaction is recorded. If the Page receives a review, photo view, or video play, those numbers are also tracked. Insights provides an aggregated number of interactions and breaks down the actions separately.

Next to this graph is a graph detailing demographic breakdown of active fans for the week. It provides the number of fans who have interacted with your Page, along with their sex and age group.

Assessing fan loyalty

A chart directly below the first measurement shows fans to unsubscribed fans across an adjustable timeline. You can also view by new fans versus removed fans, or unsubscribed fans versus re-subscribed fans. These measurements can help you gauge fan loyalty and your effectiveness at maintaining a lasting relationship with your fan base.

Gaining deeper insights

Facebook Insights also provides a monthly breakdown of fan interaction with the Page, followed by top visits by country and language. If a Page shows little fan engagement, there won't be many metrics available via Insights.

Facebook only provides demographic data, such as age and gender, or geographic data based on the user's location if there is significant interaction with your Page.

And Facebook continues to improve its Insights dashboard. In addition to adding graphs that are more detailed and separate breakouts of fan interactions, the company has devised a new Post Quality score shown on the top right of your Insights page (see Figure 10-2 to view the Post Quality score). This number, represented by 1 to 5-point star-based scale, measures how engaging your Page contributions have been to visitors over a rolling seven day period.

You can easily export your data as a CSV or Microsoft Excel (.xls) file. From your Facebook Ads page, click the Reports link and select what report you want to generate, for which period, and in what format. Click the Generate Report button and Facebook displays your report (see Figure 10-3).

Attracting more fans to your Page

Creating compelling content is central to fostering strong fan interaction. By encouraging your fans to contribute and interact with your Page, their social interactions result in news stories that in turn are seen on personal profile pages and amplify interest. Therefore, engagement begets more engagement.

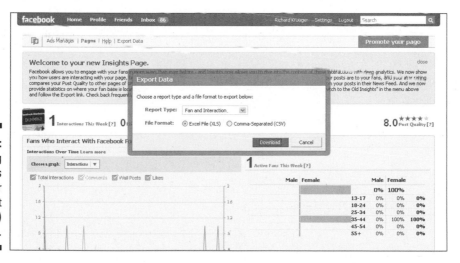

Figure 10-3: Exporting reports as CSV or Microsoft Excel (.xls) files.

The Insight tool evaluates the performance of your Page by the percentage of fans that engage with that Page (see Figure 10-3). The stars on the right of your screen indicate how your Page stacks up against similar Pages (based on similar number of fans and visitors). To increase your Post Quality score (see Figure 10-2), consider the following:

- ✓ **Contribute relevant content.** Whether it be uploading photos or videos, adding links, or writing notes, the content should be fresh and on topic. (See Chapter 6.)

- ✓ **Update your content frequently.** But you do not want to turn off your fan base by making too many posts. Many would find this annoying and bordering on spam.

- ✓ **Offer an incentive, or exclusive access to content.** To increase your fan base, host a contest (see Chapter 15), start an ad campaign (see Chapter 9), or sponsor an Event (see Chapter 8). By increasing your fan base, you're increasing the likelihood of social engagements that take place on your Page.

Chapter 11

Buying and Selling within the Marketplace

. . . .

In This Chapter

▶ Introducing the Facebook Marketplace application

▶ Using the Marketplace application

▶ Posting an item for sale

▶ Shopping for your favorite charity

▶ Managing your listings

▶ Complying with Marketplace guidelines

. . . .

*I*f you are reading this chapter, chances are you're interested in making money using the Facebook Marketplace. Facebook offers several ways to buy and sell your wares within the Facebook Platform with assorted third-party applications (apps). (See Chapter 12.) More than two million people use the Facebook Marketplace, and as that popularity grows, so do the number of apps that members can add to their profiles.

In this chapter, we introduce you to the most widely used Facebook Marketplace application, and show you how to add it to your Facebook interface. We discuss how to shop using key Marketplace features and how you can shop for your favorite charitable cause. After that, we dive into selling in the Marketplace from posting and managing a listing to complying with the Marketplace guidelines.

Getting to Know the Marketplace

The official Facebook Marketplace application is a fully integrated package that you can add via the Facebook Applications menu. Powered by Oodle, a third-party software manufacturer, the Marketplace offers an easy to use

Home page (see the "Viewing the Marketplace Home page" section, later in this chapter). The predecessor to this Marketplace was owned and operated by Facebook itself, but was not as elegant as the new solution. By enlisting the help of Oodle, Facebook has supercharged this part of its platform and opened it up to over 200 local and national sites that Oodle is affiliated with.

Oodle is also a standalone Web site and is considered one of the fastest growing classifieds networks. Oodle powers other companies' classifieds Web sites including:

- ✔ Traditional newspapers, such as The Sun, The San Diego Union-Tribune, and the New York Post
- ✔ Web site companies, such as Lycos, Local.com, and MySpace
- ✔ Nontraditional classifieds hosting sites, such as Wal-Mart

Therefore, when you post something on the Marketplace through Oodle, your listing appears on hundreds of leading media and publishing sites, which is good news for you.

The Marketplace is truly different from other popular sites like eBay or Craigslist because it integrates into the fabric of Facebook. Items that you post to the Marketplace appear on your Wall, thus allowing you to take advantage of the viral aspect of Facebook.

Facebook lets you view listings according to your default geographic location plus some distance from your location and that gives you some unique views on the Marketplace that you typically don't get with eBay or Craigslist. Also, you don't see features like Sell for a Cause or Giving It Away on a site like eBay that needs to charge for listings. Unlike eBay, however, the cost of posting a listing on the Marketplace is always free.

How you purchase items on the Marketplace is different from eBay and similar to Craigslist where you contact the seller via e-mail with the subject line of the e-mail pre-populated with the name of the listing. From there, you engage in a dialogue with the buyer and ultimately purchase the item if the price is right! Transaction payments typically use PayPal, credit cards, or cash if you meet in person.

Viewing the Marketplace Home page

The Marketplace lets you buy, sell, give things away, or ask for anything you want — from people you know in Facebook to anyone on the Oodle network. If there's a cause or charity you support, you can sell on behalf of that cause too.

The Marketplace Home page (see Figure 11-1) organizes its wares into four major categories: Items for Sale, Housing, Vehicles, and Jobs, and defaults to your Facebook geographic location. Items for Sale is the default category and Facebook lists all items that are available in your geographic location in the center of your screen.

If you click any of these key categories, then you get to the corresponding main page, which contains a more detailed list and advanced search features for that category. If you want to be more specific, you can click any of the subcategories that you see listed.

Charitable causes

Unique to the Facebook Marketplace is the Causes link where you can buy or sell items to support your favorite charities. Say you're a Grammy winning artist and you would like to raise money for the Sierra Club Foundation. You could sell autographed CDs of your music to raise money and awareness for this charity. Anyone who buys your CDs automatically donates the entire selling price to the charity.

If you don't have a preferred charity, you can search from the list on your screen. For more information, see the "Shopping for Charitable causes" section, later in this chapter.

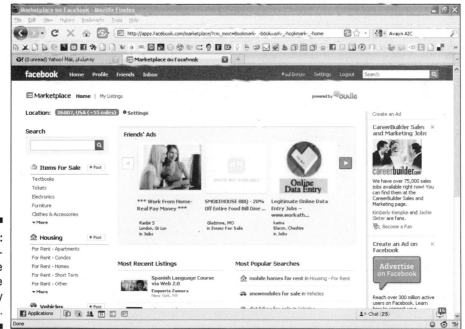

Figure 11-1:
The Market-
place
Home page
powered by
Oodle.

My Listings

My Listings screen lets you view all your listings: active, closed, or expired. For more information, click the My Listings link in the top navigation of the Marketplace. For more information, see the "Managing My Listings" section later in this chapter.

Others can find out about your listings in a few ways. When you post a listing to the Marketplace, it automatically displays on your Wall. You have several ways to share (as you do with a Facebook Page) using the Share button to send a message to your friends and fans or post to your personal profile (see Chapter 6 for more information).

Other Facebook marketplace applications

Actually, Facebook offers a few other applications you should be aware of that allow you to make money using the Facebook Platform. Some applications allow you to pull listings from outside Facebook to sell to Facebook members, and others allow you to make money via referral programs. You should be aware of (and keep an eye on) the following applications.

eBay and Facebook

The most obvious bunch of applications you should be aware of is the eBay and Facebook application. Facebook offers several applications that allow you to quickly and easily pull items you have for sale on eBay into the Facebook environment to share with your friends what you are buying, selling, and even watching on eBay. You can also update your Wall with any activity from your eBay account, such as when you buy, sell, or list an item and get or give feedback on an item.

Lemonade Stand

With about 1,000 monthly active users, Lemonade Stand allows you to make money from the sale of products you recommend to your friends. This is known as an *affiliate program*. All you need to do is add this application, search the Web for favorite stuff, and when someone purchases from your stand, you get paid. Bada bing!

iList

iList is another application that takes any classifieds listing and promotes it across your Facebook, MySpace, Twitter, FriendFeed, Pownce, and even Craigslist accounts. By adding the iList application, you can promote listings to your Facebook friends as well as manage your listings without leaving Facebook. With over 1,500 monthly active users, this application is another one to keep an eye on.

So dive in and start looking around the Marketplace.

Shopping in the Marketplace

Shopping in the Facebook Marketplace couldn't be easier with people selling everything from books to designer fashions. No matter what the product, everyone loves a bargain, and there are plenty to be had. The Facebook Marketplace represents a great opportunity for entrepreneurial individuals to sell your products directly to the retail market since there are very few major retail chains on the Marketplace at this point. In this section we discuss how to add the Marketplace application to Facebook and then how to search within the Marketplace for the items that you desire.

Adding the Marketplace App

Facebook allows you to have and bookmark up to six of your favorite Facebook apps in your bottom navigation bar. If you are new to Facebook, or don't see the Marketplace listed in your Applications menu, then you'll need to add the Marketplace app using the steps below:

1. **In the lower navigation bar, choose Applications⇨Browse More Applications. (See Figure 11-2.)**

Figure 11-2: Finding the Marketplace is easy.

Browse More Applications

2. **Type** marketplace **into the Search box and press Enter.**

   The Marketplace application by Oodle appears at the top of the results in the Applications directory. (See Figure 11-3.)

3. **Click the Marketplace icon to view the Marketplace introduction.**

4. **Click Go to Application to go to the Marketplace.**

   To find the Marketplace again, add the bookmark link to the bottom navigation bar by clicking the Marketplace link when it appears.

If you're an experienced Facebook user, you might already have a Marketplace icon located on the bottom navigation bar. If so, click that to access the Marketplace app.

Figure 11-3: Searching for the Market-place application.

Posting by category

You can post items according to four categories of listings (for more information, see "Posting a Listing" later in this chapter). Any of these listings can apply to your business, it just depends on the objective of your listing. The categories are

✔ **Sell It:** Sell items to raise cash

✔ **Sell for a Cause:** Donate the proceeds to charity

✔ **Give It Away:** Reduce waste and give it away

✔ **Ask for It:** Find something obscure that isn't displayed already

Changing your geographic location

Results are always based on your location, and in our case, the location is the USA. However, if you want to change the country or the settings of your location, you can use the Location Settings link to the right of the search box. You can narrow or broaden your search based on the number of miles that you want to surround your zip code. For countries outside the USA, you can search for items by just the country name, for example, Tanzania.

For this search, we narrowed the results to a 50-mile radius around a location (see Figure 11-4). This decreased the total listings from more than 97,000 to just over 2,400 with one click. This is quite handy to find items of interest you can go check out or even test drive if you need to.

Figure 11-4: Refined search to just 50 miles from a location.

Narrowing your search in the Marketplace

All the primary search features are built into the left navigation column and make shopping in the Marketplace easy. You can switch to a new category of items to view by using the top four links: Items for Sale, Housing, Vehicles, and Jobs. Or you can search for a specific product by typing it into the Search box. If you still haven't found what you're looking for, refine your search by clicking the subcategory you want to display. Finally, the specific listing type can be changed by scrolling down and clicking your desired option.

Using the Marketplace Search box

The broadest of searches uses the Search box at the top of the left hand navigation bar. A quick keyword search for *Clothes* shows a mix of items for sale, items sold for a cause, items that are given away, and items that people are asking for. Items can then be narrowed to just items being offered within a certain number of miles from your home or items being offered by your friends. (See Figure 11-5.)

Figure 11-5:
Clothing
items
offered by
my friends.

Finding items in a category

Searching by category is your first step to getting the results that you're looking for. The categories are Items for Sale, Housing, Vehicles, and Jobs, and some categories are clearly more popular than others.

At the time of this writing, Housing – For Rent - Apartments (see Figure 11-6) had more than 97,000 listings of 229,000 total Marketplace listings (which is 42 percent of all listings). Vehicles had over 80,000 listings (or 34 percent of all listings), Items for Sale had 33,000 listings (or 14 percent of all listings), and Jobs had the remaining 3,000 listings (or 1 percent of all listings). Over time and as this space begins to get more interesting to members, the top categories may shift.

Figure 11-6:
Searching
by
Housing –
For Rent –
Apartments.

Posting a Listing

Entering a listing in the Marketplace is fun because it's so easy. The design of the page has been simplified so that it should only take you a few minutes to enter a listing. Best of all, every listing is free for Facebook members!

Because this book is about driving your business via Facebook no matter what size your business might be, we focus on the Sell It listings. The Sell It tab is the default tab under Items for Sale, which is potentially why a majority of listings are Sell It items.

1. **On the Marketplace Home page, click the Post button next to the category you want to sell: Items for Sale, Housing, Vehicles, or Jobs.**

2. **Select the type of listing you want:**

   • *Sell It:* Sell something to make extra cash.

   • *Sell for a Cause:* Sell something and donate the proceeds to a cause.

   • *Give It Away:* Give away something you're not using.

   • *Ask for It:* Ask Facebook members to help you find something.

As you might imagine, many of the listings are the Sell It type when it comes to Items for Sale (approximately 84 percent at the time of this writing). Clearly, if you have something to sell, like a book, this is the spot for it. (See Figure 11-7.)

Using Give It Away listings might make a great advertisement for your business if you sell products or services. Why not give away a free sample or a free assessment to those near your office!

3. **Type a title in the What are you selling box, and then click post.**

   Be sure to keep your headline short and to the point by putting the name of the product or service at the beginning.

4. **Type why you're selling the item in the Why Are You Selling It? text box.**

   Many people write practical descriptions, such as, "I just need the money," but consider a more provocative answer, something that will get your listing noticed. Because this space is visible in any search results, think of it as an extension to your headline although it isn't a mandatory field.

5. **Type the price that you are asking.**

   Price is not a mandatory field. Unlike eBay, you have no way of gauging a market price for your item, especially if it's used. So consider doing a search on either a search engine or a Web site, such as eBay or Craigslist to determine fair market value of your item.

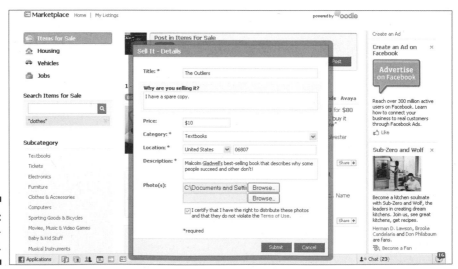

Figure 11-7: The Sell It - Details box.

6. **Choose a Category from the drop-down menu.**

   Choices range from Baby & Kid Stuff to Everything Else. If you can't find a category that best describes your item, you can always use the catch all Everything Else.

7. **Your location, derived from your profile, is filled in automatically.**

   You can change the location if you are selling something remotely or from a network different from where you are now.

8. **Type a description.**

   While the box looks like it takes about two to four lines of type, it takes well more than that, so don't feel constrained.

9. **Add up to two photos although only one is required.**

   In our example of selling a spare book, you could add the front and back cover. You can even add more photos later.

10. **Be sure to certify that you have the right to distribute the photos, and then click Submit.**

    New listings take approximately 30 minutes to be included in search results. Many listings take much less than 30 minutes to appear, but 30 minutes is the maximum.

Facebook displays a miniature version of what your listing will look like, reminding you to expect an e-mail within 30 minutes telling you that your listing has gone live. Click Continue to close that dialog box.

A screen displays and asks whether you want to publish this listing to your Facebook Wall and to the News Feed of your friends' Home pages. It includes a dialog box where you can write comments. We recommend that you publish this to your profile so your listing reaches the broadest audience possible outside the Marketplace.

Promoting your listing to your friends

After you list an item in the Marketplace, it's time to promote your listing to some friends and put the viral aspect of Facebook to work for you. Sharing your listing will get your friends engaged in promoting your item for you.

Check out the Share this Listing section in the left hand navigation column. There are plenty of ways to share your listing by publishing it to your Wall and your friends' Home pages using various social expressions such as: Like it!, Check it out!, or Share something else (see Figure 11-8). Also you can enlist your friends to Like it?, Should I buy this?, or Ask something else. Or you could just send a virtual gift to make someone's day — from any listing page!

Figure 11-8:
Commenting
on a listing.

You can also share a listing with a friend using the more traditional method of sharing via Facebook e-mail. To share your listing, go to the individual listing and click the Share button. From there you can click Send as a Message Instead and type your text. Then you can choose up to 20 of your friends by either typing their name into the Search box or using a friend List. Add a short message about your listing and click Send. (See Figure 11-9.) (See Chapter 6.)

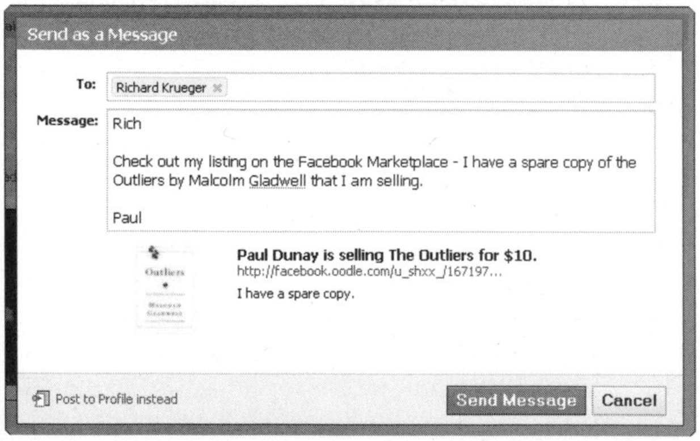

Figure 11-9:
Sharing an
item with a
friend via
Facebook
e-mail.

Promoting a listing to your profile

Use the Share button to post this item on your profile's Wall. A message then also appears on the Wall of your friends.

Start with the specific listing that you want to post, and click the Share button. From there you can add a short message about your listing and click Share. (See Figure 11-10.)

Figure 11-10:
Promoting
an item on a
profile.

Shopping by Charitable Causes

The main idea of the Find a Cause page is to let you buy or sell goods to support your favorite charity. Shopping to benefit a charitable cause is unique to the Facebook Marketplace.

At the top of your Marketplace screen, next to the Home link, click Causes to get to the Find a Cause page. Under the Marketplace logo, you can type the name or keyword of your favorite cause in the Search box. You can also specify a new geographic location or a category of causes that you would like to view, such as arts, culture, humanities, environment, animals, or religion from the drop-down lists.

On the right side of your screen, Facebook displays a Featured Cause, which is a part of the Marketplace that runs in cooperation with an independent site called Guidestar. To have your favorite cause become a Featured Cause, you need to sign up with Guidestar via the Powered by Guidestar icon at the bottom of the Find a Cause page, or by navigating to their site at www.guide star.org. (See Figure 11-11.)

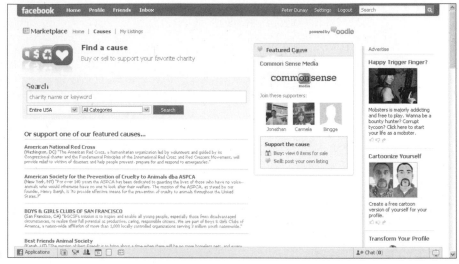

Figure 11-11: The Find a Cause page in Facebook Market-place.

Managing Your Listings

Managing your listings is made easy for you in the Marketplace. At the top of your Marketplace screen, click the My Listings link next to Causes. Facebook collects your active and inactive listings in one spot so you can promote, edit, or close them all from one location. (See Figure 11-12.)

Listings that are older than 30 days expire on their own.

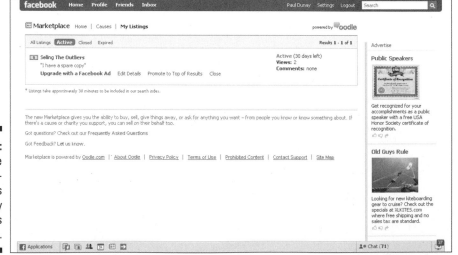

Figure 11-12: Manage your existing listings on the My Listings page.

Promoting a listing

You have three ways to promote your listings in the Marketplace: Upgrade with a Facebook Ad (see Chapter 9), use the Promote to Top of Results link to republish your listing to the top of the search results for that item every 24 hours, and share your listing with friends (see Chapter 6).

Editing a listing

After you publish your listing, editing that listing is as easy as clicking the Edit Details link contained in the listing or located under any of the listings on your My Listings page. You can make changes to the same details screen that you used to enter the listing. You can also upload added photos, if you wish. Initially, you limited your upload to just two photos, but now you can add as many as you want.

The more complex the listing, the more photos you should use to help sell it.

After you tweak your listing with the changes you desire, click Submit to make them go live. You are then directed to publish this listing to your profile. We feel there is nothing to lose by promoting a listing on your personal profile.

Closing a listing

On your My Listings page, you can close the listing after you sell it or if you decide not to sell it. In the listing view, click the Close link, which is near the Edit Details link. Answer the question, "Did you sell [your item name]?" We assume Facebook is monitoring the success of this platform so your feedback is welcome.

Abiding by Marketplace Guidelines

As you might imagine, the Facebook members who use the Marketplace are very protective of the content. Poor content reflects poorly on all of the members so it is up to everyone to police it.

When looking at an individual listing, you will find at the bottom of every listing the Report link, which gives you the ability to report it to Facebook based on whether you believe the listing to be miscategorized, fraudulent, illegal, inappropriate, spam, or unavailable. For more details on the Marketplace abuse policy, see the Terms of Use and the Prohibited Content list located in the Marketplace.

Below are some guidelines on what we feel are the most important things to keep in mind when using the Marketplace.

- ✔ **Listings must be accurate:** Be sure that your listing is as accurate as possible. Put disclaimers on a product or warnings if there is something you need to call the buyer's attention to. You don't want to be accused of fraud with your listing.

- ✔ **Only one listing of an item allowed:** Use only using one listing at a time for any given item, if you don't want to be reported for spam. If you do enter a listing twice by accident, be sure to delete one in a timely fashion.

- ✔ **Must have right to sell, lease, or rent item:** Be sure that you have the right to rent the space; otherwise, you might be reported. Remember the old saying, "I've got a bridge I can sell you"? Well, if it's not your bridge, you can't sell it on Facebook. One of the more popular categories is Housing – For Rent, which accounts for almost a third of all listings.

- ✔ **May not post inappropriate items:** Don't even think about posting a listing that is threatening to a group or individual, violent, obscene, or contains copyrighted material as inappropriate content is not tolerated. Marketplace members will report you quickly.

- ✔ **Must not promote illegal activity:** Do not promote illegal activity, such as pornography, prostitution, or drug-related activity. Marketplace members will report you.

- ✔ **All real estate listings must comply with the Fair Housing Act:** Know that the Fair Housing Act prohibits discrimination in the sale, rental, and financing of dwellings, and in other housing-related transactions, based on race, color, national origin, religion, sex, familial status (including children under the age of 18 living with parents or legal custodians, pregnant women, and people securing custody of children under the age of 18), and disability.

- ✔ **Certain items prohibited:** Don't post any item related to any of the following: nudity, pornography, drugs, threats to a group or individual, violence, obscenity, and copyrighted material, as they are strictly prohibited.

- ✔ **Parties are solely responsible:** Be responsible for your own listings and activity on the Marketplace. Every listing can be traced back to its owner, so don't publish anything you wouldn't want to see on the cover of the newspaper.

✔ **Listings are public:** Keep in mind that all listings are open to the public outside Facebook because they are part of the Oodle network. Potential buyers need to log into Facebook to respond to you and cannot see your profile (which is controlled by your privacy settings on your Profile page). (See Chapter 2 for information about privacy settings.)

✔ **Exercise caution in providing contact or personal information:** Be cautious about providing contact and personal information, because all listings are public. Use the features that are built into the platform, such as the Contact button under your picture or the Wall on your listing, for all communications.

Part IV
Riding the Facebook Viral Wave

The 5th Wave   By Rich Tennant

DARRYL PREPARES TO ENGAGE WITH THE AQUA INTERFACE PAGE

In this part . . .

Despite the great ideas you've gotten so far from the book, there are strategies and tactics that can make your Facebook presence even stronger! In this part, we discuss Facebook applications that can help you form a deeper engagement with your Facebook clients and then learn how to best leverage the Facebook API and platform for branding.

You'll find out how to host your own Facebook contest and conduct surveys that can give you insight into your target market. Finally, we show you how to extend the Facebook platform to your own Web site through Facebook Connect and tap into the viral features that have helped make Facebook so successful.

Chapter 12

Dressing Up Your Facebook Page with Applications

In This Chapter

▶ Introducing Facebook applications

▶ Finding and adding applications to your Facebook Page

▶ Advertising in applications

▶ Developing your own applications

*F*acebook applications (apps) have become powerful tools for marketers. They can serve a variety of functions when installed on your Facebook profile and/or Page and are a great way to add some sizzle to your business's Facebook presence. In fact, Facebook apps are becoming so popular that 70 percent of Facebook members regularly interact with them every month.

Facebook now lists more than 52,000 apps in the Application Directory. Individuals and third-party companies created the majority of them. Facebook allows anyone to build an app that works on the Facebook Platform (as long as the app adheres to the Facebook developer guidelines). Although many of these apps are not intended for business use, such as games, trivia quizzes, and other time-wasting pursuits, the number of apps designed to address specific business needs are increasing.

We discuss how to create a Facebook Page in Chapter 4, and Facebook apps can now help bring your Page to life. Whether adding a presentation via the SlideShare app or posting content from a blog you write or admire via the Simple RSS app, apps are a key ingredient in customizing your Facebook Page and are becoming an important advertising and branding vehicle within Facebook.

Exploring Applications

Facebook apps are software modules that you can install on your Facebook profile or Page that adds a unique functionality that can further engage your audience with your brand. Apps can take on many different forms, from video players to business cards to contest solutions. Facebook offers countless apps for marketers that provide business solutions and promote the business enterprise. Here are a few examples of what apps can do for you:

- ✔ **FedEx Launch a Package app:** Send photos, documents, and other large computer files to a friend's Inbox.

- ✔ **YouTube Video Box app:** Import your favorite videos and add them to your Page for all to see.

- ✔ **The Visa Business Network app:** Make connections with other professionals and promote your business (See Figure 12-1) through other professionals.

For a list of our favorite business apps, see Chapter 19.

Figure 12-1:
The Visa Business Network lets you network with other professionals within Facebook.

Finding an app

Facebook created a directory to help you find an app that might appeal to you and/or your business. To get to the Application Directory, choose Applications➪Browse More Applications in the lower navigation bar.

The Facebook Application Directory does a good job in providing quick and easy access to more than 52,000 apps in its library. The recently redesigned directory highlights several apps that Facebook recognizes as best in class on a rotating basis. Lower on the directory is a list of recommended apps. You can also search apps by keyword, application name, or type (see Figure 12-2). Clicking the Business category in the left column brings up a good selection of business-related apps. You can also click the Page link in the lower left column to view specific apps that install on Pages.

The bottom half of the directory is the Recent Activity from Friends section, which shows stories generated by the apps at key points of your friend's interactions (for example, filling out a survey) leveraging the Facebook News Feed technology. Stories that your fans see on their Home page let them discover new apps that their friends are using.

Figure 12-2:
You can search for apps in the Application Directory.

Adding an app

After you identify an app of interest, you can click the link to view the app's Page. Much like other Pages, the app's Page offers a Wall, company info, reviews, discussions, and boxes, and allows for some degree of customization. You can even become a fan of an app via its Page.

From the app's Page, click the Go to Application button in the left column. Facebook then displays an installation page where you permit access to the app (see Figure 12-3) into your Facebook Page or profile. It's that easy.

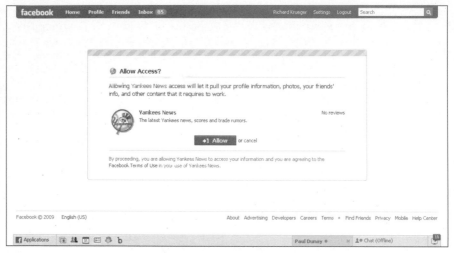

Figure 12-3:
Adding an app to your profile or Page is as easy as clicking the Allow button.

Some apps are designed for consumers, and therefore, can only be installed on profiles. Other apps are designed more for businesses, although you can install them on either your profile or Page. If you have more than one Page, the Allow Access page lists the various Pages and asks you on which Page you wish to install the app.

Deleting an app

To delete an application, simply choose Applications⇨Edit Applications on the bottom left navigation bar. You're taken to the Application Settings page, where you can simply click the X to the right of the app that you want to delete. Facebook displays a pop-up window that states if you remove the app, it can no longer have access to your data and will be removed from your profile, bookmarks, and Apps page. Click Remove in the bottom of the pop-up window to delete the app.

Some Facebook apps, like video, notes, or photos, cannot be removed. These are instrumental to the Facebook experience and Facebook has developed these internally.

Managing your apps

You can adjust your application settings by choosing Settings⇨Application Settings on the top navigation bar. Here, you'll find all the controls to manage your apps. When on the Application Settings page, you can sort your apps according to the drop-down menu on the top right. Views include apps you've recently interacted with (over the past month), your bookmarked apps, apps on your profile, authorized apps, apps that are allowed to post your interactions, and apps that you've granted additional permissions to.

Following is a run-down of key controls within apps:

- ✔ **Bookmarks:** Access your apps using the links in the Applications menu on the bottom left navigation bar. The top six bookmarked apps also appear as icons alongside the Applications menu. Bookmarks make it easy to access an app at any time. Please note, there will always be six bookmarked apps. As a new bookmark is added, the bottom one will slide off.

- ✔ **Authorizations:** Specify who receives your news stories about a specific app by choosing Settings⇨Applications on the top right navigation bar in Facebook. Additional Permissions lets you control stories published to your Wall that relate to the app. (See Figure 12-4.)

- ✔ **Wall Permissions:** Specify the types of stories related to these apps that you want to appear.

- ✔ **Additional Permissions:** Adjust when Facebook allows an app to e-mail you or access your data when you're offline.

- ✔ **External Web site Settings:** Change your settings for Web sites here.

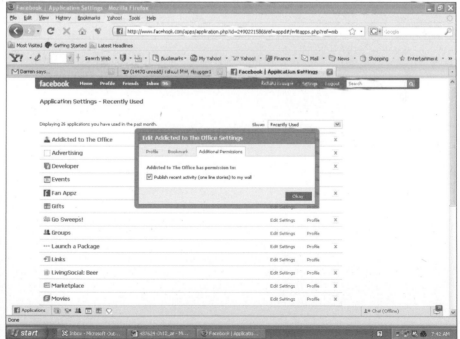

Figure 12-4:
You can manage your apps from within the Application Settings.

Setting privacy controls

Facebook apps can generate news stories based on your interaction with the app. If you spend lots of time playing Facebook games, for example, you might want to pay attention to your app's privacy settings. There are a number of ways that application developers can create *triggers*, actions that generate news stories. Following are a few triggers to keep in mind when you interact with any apps:

- ✔ **News Feed:** Takes advantage of a member's News Feed and publishes stories to it (see Figure 12-5).

- ✔ **Privacy Settings:** Lets you grant approval to publish stories, add or remove the app's profile box, and control who sees them.

- ✔ **Alerts:** Sends alerts, or notifications, to a member's e-mail. Permission must be granted before a member can receive e-mail. Furthermore, the member who generates the action must approve before the e-mail is sent.

- ✔ **Requests:** Generates requests, which appear on the top right of a member's Home page. These requests are typically triggered by a member's friend, and often request confirmation (for example, John requests that you join him for a game of Scrabble).

Figure 12-5:
Facebook applications that generate news stories can leverage the viral effect of the social network.

Advertising on Facebook Applications

With members spending so much time interacting with Facebook apps, it didn't take long for the more popular apps to start selling and displaying ads. Developers suddenly had a lucrative revenue stream, while providing marketers with a highly captive and well-defined, app-hungry audience.

This new ad medium also spawned a new ad model — pay-per-install. Now, companies with their own apps could advertise on other apps, and pay only when the viewer installs the advertised app. Often, these pay-per-install ads are presented as recommendations, for example, "People who installed this app, also enjoyed these." And, many times, they appear on a landing page outside of Facebook where terms aren't dictated according to the Facebook policies.

With apps, advertisers could closely align their brand with a useful, per-haps even complimentary social activity (see Figure 12-6). Companies like Blockbuster, for example, could associate their brand with an app such as Flixster, a popular movie trivia game enjoyed by more than 17 million active monthly users.

Application advertising is a good way to ensure that a particular branded app gets enough installs, which in turn, generates News Feed stories and fuels viral growth. If you're willing to pay $1.00 per install on 50,000 users (a $50,000 ad budget), the amplified effect of attracting new users could signifi-cantly lower your total cost per user (CPU).

Figure 12-6: Some applications carry ads to incentivize you to download other applications.

Understanding Facebook as a Platform

Facebook opened up its Platform, or operating system, for developers to create engaging apps. Facebook maintains extensive resources for develop-ers, from online tutorials to script libraries to bug reporting tools, and does not charge a development fee. More than one million developers have signed on to develop for the Facebook Platform.

Anyone can register to become a Facebook app developer (see Chapter 15), but it helps to have a good amount of technical know-how. If you plan to develop your own app, you should be well versed in PHP or other popular coding languages, including Ruby on Rails, JavaScript, or Python. You should have application management skills and understand the fundamentals of Web hosting.

Many businesses are starting to take advantage of the Facebook Platform and creating customized apps, also known as branded apps. They can be developed relatively inexpensively and are a good way to get exposure for a company if the app goes viral, spreading to many members. From large media companies, such as MTV and CNN, to small nonprofit organizations, such as Save a Dog (see Figure 12-7), which has more than 32,000 monthly users, companies big and small are creating customized apps to get in front of their Facebook community.

Figure 12-7: DogTime. com's Save a Dog app lets players earn points while saving dogs.

The Facebook Platform serves as a self-contained operating system unto itself. The API (application programming interface) extends that operating system to developers, allowing them to tap into a member's social graph (connections, information, location, and so on.) and drives social interactions. The underlying programming language that Facebook uses is dubbed FBML, giving homage to HTML, the common Internet language protocol.

Checking out resources for app developers

Facebook provides plenty of resources within its Facebook Developers page for both the novice and the experienced developer. To get there, scroll down to the bottom of your Facebook screen, and then click the Developers link. At the top of the next screen, you'll find links to Documentation that tells you how to develop a Facebook app, as well as Community that tells you where to go to interact with other developers.

Brand marketers must think virally while developing apps that motivate and engage the member. Often, this can take several design iterations to get it right.

If you're thinking about creating a customized app, whether you develop it yourself, work with an independent developer, or work with an app development studio, it's good to review the Facebook Developers page. For experienced developers, plenty of tools are available, including PHP Client Libraries, Debugging Tools, and information on various Hosting Services. (See Figure 12-8.)

Figure 12-8: Facebook provides ample resources for application developers.

Developing apps using WYSIWYG apps

Facebook offers several tools that provide a What You See is What You Get (WYSIWYG) environment to application development. With little or no technical skills, these apps promise that you'll have a fully functioning application up in no time. The Social App Studio (see Figure 12-9), which you can find in the Facebook Application Directory, brings a template approach to some of the most popular types of apps, such as gift giving.

Figure 12-9: Social App Studio lets you build a Facebook app with little or no programming knowledge.

Chapter 13

Hosting Your Own Facebook Contest

So, you've taken the time to create a Facebook Page to promote your company (see Chapter 4). But once you build it, will they come?

You need to give people a reason to visit your Page. But what can you do to cut through the clutter and attract a Facebook fan base? Increasingly, marketers are turning to contests for the answer.

Companies that host contests and giveaways have been able to attract hundreds-of-thousands of entries and fans, as we'll show you. This chapter discusses how you can use contests to motivate and grow your audience by promoting brand awareness and building community. We then show you how you can host your own Facebook contest.

Everyone Loves a Contest

Contests and giveaways have traditionally played a vital role in consumer marketing. From cereal companies to fashion retailers, automobile dealers to cosmetic companies, the promise of winning something of value for free is a tremendous lure. Whether backed by a media campaign, promoted on a product's packaging, or announced at an employee sales meeting, contests have the power to motivate, incentivize, and drive engagement.

And, the same incentives that have served marketers BFB (Before Facebook) still apply on Facebook. Contests with high-value prizes tend to be more active. Celebrity appeal and limited edition offerings always help, too. But for marketers who don't have access to costly prizes, you can still offer an appropriate reward. I have been known to fill out a form for the chance to win a tee shirt, but it was a really cool tec shirt.

The best part about marketing on Facebook is that you don't have to be a major brand to host a successful contest (although it doesn't hurt). And, you don't have to have a boatload of money to pull off a successful contest (although that doesn't hurt, either). Anyone with a Facebook Page can create and promote a contest. While Facebook does not offer a contest application, you can easily improvise and promote your contest on your Wall. Or, check out some of the third-party contest applications (apps) to find a solution that works best for your promotion.

Win a Prize by Wildfire Interactive, Inc. is a free Facebook contest app that provides a direct solution for marketers looking to offer a contest or give-away on their Facebook Page. Win a Prize provides everything you need to create and host a contest on your Facebook Page (see Figure 13-1). From your bottom navigation bar, choose Applications⇨Browse More Applications, and type Win a Prize in the Facebook Search box to find and install the app.

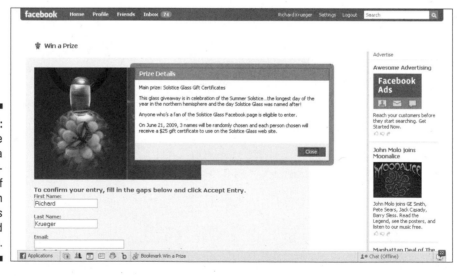

Figure 13-1: Win a Prize offers a build-it-yourself approach to contests and giveaways.

Using contests to promote your brand

When you offer a good incentive, word travels. On Facebook, when you offer a good incentive, word reverberates off friends. When members interact with the contest by uploading videos or images, answering questions, or becoming a fan of your Page, it generates News Feed stories, amplifying the word-of-mouth effect. A contest or giveaway promotion can be a very viral vehicle to ignite fan engagement with your Facebook Page.

When Neutrogena launched their Facebook Page in April 2009, they created a contest to build brand awareness and drive the key female, teen audience to their Page. The Fresh Faces contest, which was held in conjunction with Teen Vogue magazine, helped the brand attract more than 700 fans to its Facebook Page (see Figure 13-2). The winner earned a chance to be a contributing beauty editor for a Neutrogena advertorial on TeenVogue.com.

Figure 13-2: Neutrogena teamed with Teen Vogue to launch the Fresh Faces contest.

Using contests to appeal to everyone's competitive streak

Everyone loves being a winner. And, the best thing about winning is the bragging rights that go along with it. Contests generate word-of-mouth buzz because folks like to one-up their friends. This basic human trait is the motivating force behind some of the most popular Facebook contests.

Contests and giveaways can leverage the competitive nature of man (and woman) to drive engagement. Contests often employ a gaming element in which being the high scorer is the incentive to motivate someone.

Take Adobe, who wanted to reach the elusive college student market with its Adobe Student Editions, so they provided steep discounts of up to 80 percent on popular Adobe software for students. With the help of the interactive agency, Traction, the company developed a game app called Real or Fake (see Figure 13-3) in which users had to determine whether a photo was fake or real, underscoring the quality of its Adobe Photoshop imaging software. The application was featured on the Adobe Facebook Page.

Adobe engaged in a targeted ad campaign to reach interested college students. The game caught on because it was a fun and easy-to-play casual gaming experience. Of those that played, 6 percent clicked the Buy Now link at the end of the game. It also incorporated a simple Share button, in which 6 percent of players sent an invite to their friends, adding an additional point of interaction to encourage viral sharing. By the end of the competition, the Adobe Facebook Page welcomed more than 6,000 new fans.

Figure 13-3:
The Adobe Real or Fake Facebook interactive game gained the company 6,000 new fans.

Using contests to drive traffic to your Web site

Smart marketers leverage their Facebook contests to drive traffic to their Web site or other special landing pages outside of Facebook. Taking a hub-and-spoke approach, many companies are building communities across a number of social media hubs — from Facebook to Twitter to YouTube to Flickr — and leveraging each network to build a groundswell of interested consumers. Figure 13-4 shows you the Victoria's Secret promotion of a Free Limited Edition Bling Panty.

Figure 13-4: The Victoria's Secret Limited Edition Bling Panty giveaway.

Using contests to build community

Contests are ideal for attracting and engaging a community of like-minded people around your Page. They can serve as crucial building blocks in your Facebook brand strategy. Therefore, you need to consider a long-term approach rather than a one-off promotion in which you may see a short-lived spike in traffic but little overall affect on brand engagement. (See Chapter 5 to develop a marketing plan.)

MomLogic, a community-driven Web service, features contests front-and-center on its Facebook Page with prizes specially chosen to attract an audience of young mothers (see Figure 13-5). The Page even integrates a WIN IT! tab summarizing the current contests.

Figure 13-5: MomLogic builds a community of young mothers.

Hosting Your Own Facebook Contest

Facebook offers a compelling environment from which to host a contest or giveaway on your Page. You can use your Page as a starting point with a link to your Web site for contest entry details, or have the entire contest contained within the Facebook community.

Contests can be very creative and challenging, or simply require a single yes or no answer. They can incentivize users to upload a video, or simply complete a contact form. Some contests require a panel of esteemed judges to determine the winner; others select winners randomly. Still, other contests allow the users themselves to vote for the outcome.

Although contests are as unique as the companies that host them, we can offer you some tips that can improve your chances of success. Following are some best practices for creating Facebook contests and giveaways:

✔ **Offer an attractive prize.** The more attractive the prize, the more response you get. A box of Cracker Jacks isn't going to garner much interest. For a prize to be attractive, though, it doesn't necessarily have to cost a lot. The best prizes tend to be those that money can't buy — such as a chance to meet a celebrity, to participate in a TV commercial, or to attend a product's pre-release party.

✔ **Use your existing customers and contacts to start the ball rolling.** Getting those initial entries has always been the toughest part of running a Facebook contest. This is when you need to reach into your network of family and friends. Reach out to your mailing list of customers with a friendly invitation. Promote it to your Twitter followers via LinkedIn and MySpace. Wherever you have contacts, use whatever social network, e-mail exchange, or instant messenger you have to get them to participate.

✔ **Cross-promote via your Web site.** Facebook contests need to be promoted across all of your channels to gain maximum participation. That includes your Web site. Adding a promotional banner with a link to your Facebook Page is a good start. But, you can do so much more to promote your contest! Promote your contest on your packaging. Issue a press release via one of the many news wire services. Add a message to your phone answering system. The possibilities are endless.

✔ **Keep it simple.** This goes for all aspects of a contest. Don't overcomplicate the rules. The fewer the questions on a form, the higher the rate of completion. Keep first prize a single, prized item and several smaller second place prizes. And remember, the fewer the clicks to enter the contest, the better.

✔ **Don't set the bar too high.** If you're asking the participants for an original creation, keep the requirements to a minimum. For example, don't place a minimum word count on an essay contest. Or, don't require a video for the first round of submissions because videos are perceived as a lot of work.

✔ **Run promotions for at least one month.** Your contest should run for at least a month. Word-of-mouth marketing requires time. The more time you promote the contest, the more potential entries you get.

✔ **Integrate with media campaign.** Facebook ads are an ideal complement to any contest. By combining a Facebook ad campaign with a contest, you'll maximize the viral effect and amplify the number of engagements.

✔ **Make it fun, interesting, and uniquely you.** The main thing to keep in mind when planning a Facebook contest is that members want to be entertained. Contests should offer an outlet to self-expression, engage members and encourage them to share with friends, and communicate something unique about your brand.

Facebook hosts contest to reward best application developers

To fuel the Facebook developer community, Facebook sponsored a contest to find and cash incentivize the best Facebook developers. The contest, held in conjunction with the fbFund (a venture-backed investment fund providing grants of $25K to $100K to Facebook entrepreneurs), attracted more than 600 developers who submitted entries, which was narrowed down to the top 25, who were then invited to submit videos for a public vote.

The entry requirements included a one-minute video, three to five screenshots, some basic information about the company, and a link to the working app. The public vote received nearly 200,000 votes. Almost 100,000 people installed finalists' apps. Thousands of people contributed their opinions on the entries.

To promote the competition, Facebook undertook a public relations campaign. There was no advertising to support the contest. There was also a powerful driving force behind the word-of-mouth campaign, which relied on the entrants themselves to use their networks to encourage their users, contacts, and friends to vote for them.

Ironically, the development firm, Wildfire Interactive, Inc., was among the winners for their Win a Prize Facebook contest-building app, which Facebook used to set up the very contest. Wildfire offers a do-it-yourself contest maker solution that allows users to create a Facebook contest and post it to their Facebook Page (see Chapter 4) in a matter of minutes.

Wildfire Interactive has come a long way since its Win a Prize contest app was first unveiled. The service now enables companies to integrate a Become a Fan link right into their contest entry form. You can also offer prizes that can be shared among groups of friends (for example, a trip to Vegas for you and four friends or concert tickets for you and five friends), so that entrants have a reason to invite their friends and to encourage their friends to sign up for the promotion. The system automatically notifies entrants (via Facebook notifications) when their friends accept their invitation and sends a reminder if they don't have enough friends signed up.

Wildfire also offers the ability to distribute coupons/giveaway vouchers in addition to sweepstakes and user contests and the ability to simultaneously run promotions across their Web site using a micro site that's automatically integrated with Facebook Connect (see Chapter 15) and a Facebook Page, as well as other social networks, including MySpace and Hi-5, for a truly integrated contest across a company's multiple Web-based points-of-presence.

Chapter 14

Surveying the Crowd

● ●

● ●

*T*he power of Facebook is in the size of its community. As you know by now, there are hundreds of millions of users in the Facebook network. If you and your company want to tap into the wisdom of this crowd, you're going to need to understand how to do it.

As the membership to Facebook grows, you have an opportunity to gather information from some of the most connected people on the Web. You can get hundreds or even thousands of completed surveys with lots of data, if you play it right. In this chapter, we discuss how to use Facebook for research, and then we get into the finer points of creating your own survey tools using Facebook applications (apps).

Gathering Data through Surveys

A survey is the most widely used method for collecting data in market research today. You can conduct a survey by mail, e-mail, telephone, personal interview, Web site, focus groups, or other methods. The questionnaire is one of the more common methods for collecting data from a survey and is helpful in learning about the attitudes and behaviors of your target audience. The response rate on your survey can depend on the content that you include in it and where you choose to conduct your survey.

Many companies that create surveys for market research pay people who fill them out, or even give them another kind of incentive to complete the survey. Some people like using surveys as fun, online viral activities. Surveys are a great way to share information with your friends, whether by e-mail or embedded in social networking sites like Facebook. There is probably no quicker and easier way to gain quantifiable data than through an online survey!

You have a few ways to tap into the collective wisdom of the Facebook crowd. But before you dive in, you may want to think about how to engage the Facebook audience with your survey.

Facebook members generally like to stay within the Facebook environment, so it's up to you to play by their rules as much as possible. Plenty of low-to-no-cost survey tools reside outside of Facebook on the Web, but we suggest using an application within Facebook that you can add as a new tab to your Page (see Chapter 4), which also has its own URL if you want to invite your external customers to sign in to Facebook and take the survey.

If you send your survey to folks outside Facebook, they'll need to sign up for Facebook to view it, if they aren't already a member (see Chapter 1).

Here are a few basic tips when dealing with surveys:

✔ To make it easier for Facebook members to spread the word virally, keep your survey exclusive to the Facebook community. Plus, having data exclusive to Facebook can be attractive to the media.

✔ To include people outside of Facebook, you might consider running parallel surveys — one inside Facebook and one outside Facebook — to draw conclusions between the two.

✔ To run your survey from your own business Web site, you might consider using OpenID or Facebook Connect (see Chapter 15) to make it easy for members to connect.

Defining Your Goals

Whatever your business is, start by identifying your goals, and then write a hypothesis of what you want to achieve with your data. Make sure that you decide how many completed surveys would make your research a success. Following are some possible goals:

✔ Data that you can use to validate a new product or service launch, such as: If we produced a new type of widget. Would you buy it?

✔ Data that you can use to produce white papers or for the press, such as: Would you recommend your bank to your best friend?

✔ Data that you can use for business development, such as: What is your next big IT project?

✔ Data that you can use for benchmarking, such as: What is the average time it takes your call center to respond to an e-mail?

✔ Just for the fun of it! Surveys can certainly help engage your users.

Your goal in conducting a survey is to get as many completed surveys as possible. The number of completed surveys that many studies aim for is 100 or more. Any fewer than that is sometimes considered statistically invalid if you are trying to use the data with the press or in a magazine.

Checking Out Facebook Survey Apps

No matter what kind of survey you choose, a number of apps have sprung up to satisfy the needs of marketers to research the Facebook community into the next century.

To find these apps, choose Applications⇨Browse More Applications from the lower navigation bar. Type "polls" into the Search box, and then press Enter. (See Figure 14-1.) Poll applications appear and you can now select a polling app by clicking its link.

Figure 14-1: Searching for polls in the Applications Directory.

Here are a few of our favorite poll apps that you can find in Facebook, along with a short description of what they do.

- ✔ **Polls:** Polls is a popular application that lets marketers tap into the power of their Pages and profiles by creating their own custom polls. Created by Context Optional, polls are easy to create and Facebook displays the results using rich and colorful graphics. (See Figure 14-2.)

- ✔ **Daily Experience Survey:** Posts a new survey of 10 questions daily. The surveys range from serious to seriously funny (see Figure 14-3). Facebook users can post the app to their profile as a means of making their profile more sticky and engaging. The results are also posted to the profile and you can link to others who answered the same way as you. Sometimes there's an incentive associated with the survey, but not every time. To find this app, search for "Daily Survey" in the Applications Directory.

- ✔ **YouGov:** Delivers surveys ranging from government policies to retail, fashion, and beyond (see Figure 14-4). YouGov members are typically paid for their opinion so you need to have a modest budget to work with them. YouGov is based in the UK, which can help if you want a global audience response. To find this app, search for "YouGov" in the Application Directory.

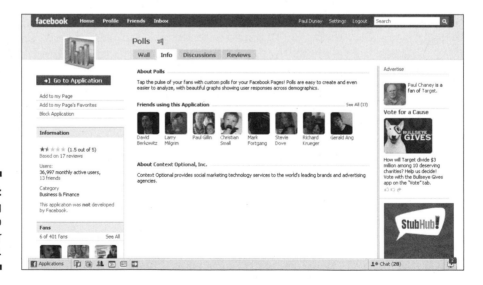

Figure 14-2:
Viewing Polls to tap into your fans.

✔ **SocialToo:** When you want fast response survey data that you can publish quickly in a report or on your Web site, this Web-based tool can provide short bursts of survey data (see Figure 14-5). SocialToo has a very elegant user interface and works well with Facebook. To find this application, search for "Social Too" in the Application Directory.

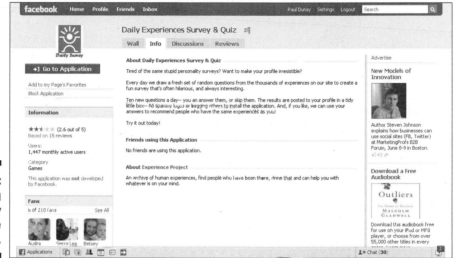

Figure 14-3: Checking out the Daily Experience Survey.

Figure 14-4: Having more of a government focus with YouGov.

✔ **Quibblo:** Provides a variety of free survey and quiz templates that you can quickly customize and post directly to your Facebook account. Quibblo is a Web-based tool (see Figure 14-6) that integrates well with social networks, such as Facebook, MySpace, Bebo, and Hi5, as well as a variety of blogging platforms including Blogger, WordPress, and TypePad. To access Quibblo, go to the Quibblo Web site.

Figure 14-5: Using a short survey tool like SocialToo.

Figure 14-6: Checking out Quibblo to survey any social network.

Creating a Facebook Survey

Creating and designing a survey is a fine art honed by marketers for years. So, you do not need to reinvent the wheel since you can find so many resources to help you. Following are some basics to help you create a winning survey.

- ✔ **Keep it short.** When drafting your survey, you should brainstorm as many questions as you can to be sure that you cover all the bases. Then go back over the questions and mark the questions in three categories: essential, useful, and nice to have. Keep the survey to essential questions only, and as few of the useful questions as possible.

  There is an inverse relationship between the number of questions in your survey and the number of complete surveys you will receive, so the shorter the survey the better!

- ✔ **Write down the expected outcome.** This trick is critical for helping you decide whether a question is essential. Try to write the expected press release headline, such as "Nine out of ten dentists prefer Crest to any other toothpaste." It not only helps you qualify the question for inclusion in the survey, but also gives you a frame of reference to understand how well you know the audience. If there is a huge gap, you might want to host a discussion on your Wall about it!

- ✔ **Start with your best question.** We say this for two reasons.

  1. If you're going to get some incomplete survey data, then be sure you get your best question answered up front; don't save it until the end of the survey.

  2. Start with your most interesting question to draw in the survey taker. This way you capture their interest and you can move them toward the harder questions you saved for the end.

- ✔ **Don't sound like a survey.** Try not to sound overly complicated or use big fluffy words; use simple words that are easy to understand. An example of overly complicated wording would be, "What is the approximate frequency of your shopping behavior when it comes to the purchase of toothpaste?" A better question would be, "How many times did you buy toothpaste in the last month?"

- ✔ **Keep the choices to a minimum.** We recommend no more than five choices per question. Whether you are ranking an attribute from not important to highly important or presenting five multiple-choice options, try to keep the number of choices down so your completed survey rate goes up!

Setting a privacy policy

Just a note on privacy, some people feel very comfortable revealing personal details online that they would never divulge in real life. The anonymous interfaces of the Web lull people into a false sense of security. As the administrator of the survey, it is up to you to act responsibly with this data and never cross the line in connecting it to a profile or quoting someone when they haven't given you permission.

Facebook is a very powerful tool, even more powerful than Google in some ways because the profile data on Facebook members is so accessible. Because of this, we strongly recommend that you craft a strong privacy policy and publish this with your survey.

Promoting your survey

After you create a survey on Facebook, you need to promote it. In this section, we discuss how to promote your survey and keep the energy up around it so that you maximize the number of completed forms.

After you launch the survey, the hard work of communicating that it is live and open for business kicks in and becomes a never ending process until you feel you've reached the desired number of completed forms.

Announcing your survey to fans

Facebook makes it easy to tell all your fans about the new survey, so why not take advantage of it? You can post a quick update about the survey in the News Feed for your Page and send messages directly to all your fans to get their attention (see Chapter 6). You can also keep the updates coming while you get more and more completed surveys. Don't be afraid to ask for help from your friends and fans by posting, "71 Completes! We just need 29 more!"

Announcing your survey to external clients

You can always invite your existing customers via e-mail to take your survey. If this sounds like the path you want to take, you have two ways to accomplish this:

- ✔ **Use your personal or business e-mail account.** Because Pages have their own URL, you can copy the URL into your message, inviting customers to log in to Facebook and take your survey.

  Not everyone in your database is a member of Facebook, which means non-Facebook members need to join Facebook to take your survey (see Chapter 2).

- ✔ **Use the Facebook e-mail system.** You have less control over how it looks from a branding perspective, but it is very consistent with all the other Facebook experiences that your fans are already having.

Chapter 15

Reaching out Further with Facebook Connect

*F*acebook is all about connecting with friends and, in the case of Facebook Pages for business, fans. Although Facebook has previously focused on containing the experience within the Facebook community, the company has recently launched Facebook Connect to bring many of the viral marketing benefits of Facebook to third-party Web sites, devices, and applications (apps). Facebook Connect represents the evolution of data portability, allowing a site owner to bring many of the same features that fans are familiar with on Facebook to your Web site.

In this chapter, we show you how Facebook Connect can expand your customer base by drawing fans from your Facebook Page to your Web site and attracting other Facebook members.

Introducing Facebook Connect

Since launching in December 2008, more than 15,000 Web sites, devices, and apps have implemented Facebook Connect — and the list is growing. Facebook Connect is a new feature that extends Facebook Platform to other Web sites and offers members the ability to connect their Facebook identity, friends, and privacy settings to a Facebook Connect-enabled Web site. There is no charge for Web site owners to integrate Facebook Connect, although there is rumor of a Facebook ad network in the works serving ads across these sites.

For now, one thing is for sure, savvy marketers are using Facebook Connect in unique, compelling, and engaging ways by providing members with a way of sharing with their friends and fostering community. Figure 15-1 shows a Facebook Connect implementation on the Web guide Citysearch, which allows you to publish reviews to your Facebook profile.

Figure 15-1:
A Facebook
Connect
implemen-
tation on
local Web
guide
Citysearch.

Facebook Connect allows Facebook to extend its influence on the Web at large. By turning its social network outside in, it's empowering tens-of-thousands of Web sites and blogs, both big and small, to make use of many of the same features that have made Facebook the fastest growing social network on the planet. And it's proving to be a successful strategy.

The main point to adding Facebook Connect is to encourage members to interact with your Web site in ways that generate stories in Facebook. It's this seamless integration between Facebook Connect partner sites and Facebook News Feed stories that can help make your site viral, that is, spread very quickly within a specific group of friends or to a larger demographic.

Here are four more reasons your organization should add Facebook Connect to its Web site:

✔ Allows your visitors to effortlessly connect their Facebook account and profile information with your Web site.

✔ Offers site owners access to fans Facebook profiling data, such as name, location, age, and so on, to provide deeper insights into your site visitors.

✔ Provides your visitors with an easy way to find and interact with other Facebook friends who also visit your Web site.

✔ Leverages Facebook News Feeds as a way to share and promote your other members' actions on your site with their Facebook friends, increasing word-of-mouth buzz and the likelihood of more Facebook visitors.

Like all platform extensions, Facebook Connect does require some sophistication on the part of the Web site owner. Although a number of tutorials are available, via Facebook and third-party Web sites, we recommend that an experienced Web developer integrate the code that's necessary to connect Facebook Connect to your Web site.

Flashing your Facebook badge

One of the advantages of integrating Facebook Connect with your Web site is that it eliminates the need for a Facebook member to have to go through a new registration process to access your site. A simple Facebook ID and password is sufficient for access.

Members are able to connect to your Web site using their Facebook ID and password via a trusted authentication process. This ensures the member that your Web site is a trusted environment, one in which the member maintains total control over the permissions granted. This layer of authentication guarantees the user that no more information will be shared than is allowed according to their Facebook settings, providing a comfort level necessary to engage with the site.

Confirming a member's identity

When you create a Facebook account, you use your real name and profile information. Facebook Connect allows members to bring their real identities with them when visiting a Facebook Connect partner Web site. This includes basic contact information, a profile picture, name, network(s), friends, photos, events, groups, and other relevant information included in your profile. Blogs don't typically sport a log in, but the popular tech blog TechCrunch (see Figure 15-2) was one of the first to integrate Facebook Connect as a way to get readers to do just that by using their Facebook account info.

Figure 15-2:
Popular
tech blog
TechCrunch
was one of
the first to
integrate
Facebook
Connect.

Keeping connected with friends

Facebook is enjoying tremendous growth for one central reason — it satisfies peoples' need to stay connected with their friends and family. Facebook Connect extends that capability to partner Web sites so users can continue to stay connected, even when they're not on Facebook. In this way, Facebook Connect allows users to take their friends with them. This identity portability is what Facebook Connect is all about.

Developers are adding a wide range of rich social experiences to their sites via Facebook Connect. From alerting visitors about Facebook friends who already have accounts to distributing stories, status updates, comments, and profile pictures to location-aware content, Facebook Connect partners are building better Web sites by tapping into their site visitors' social graphs and extending many of the same activities they've come to rely on within Facebook.

Increasing your Web site's visibility

One of the biggest benefits for Web site owners of adding Facebook Connect is the increased visibility among Facebook members. When Facebook members sign in to your site, their actions generate News Feed stories that have the potential of driving more visitors to you. With News Feeds, Facebook creates a highly viral environment in which your Facebook visitors serve as a viral agent, or an online evangelist, influencing their friends' actions. Video sharing site Joost allows you to share what you're watching with Facebook friends via the Facebook Connect implementation (see Figure 15-3).

Anytime a member interacts with a Facebook Connect partner site, a news story is generated (depending upon that user's privacy settings), which can appear in their friends' News Feed. Marketers need to encourage users to engage in social acts through clever prompts, such as, "Write a review and let everyone know what you think."

Getting Started with Facebook Connect

In its simplest form, Facebook Connect can be added to most existing sites with just a few lines of code, and plug-ins are available for many content management systems and blogging platforms, such as Drupral, TypePad, and WordPress. By adding Facebook Connect to your Web site, any Facebook member can use their Facebook account log-in information (that is, e-mail and password) to seamlessly log in to your Web site (or any other Facebook Connect-enabled Web site).

Connecting Facebook to your Web site

Facebook Connect behaves a lot like a Facebook app. Web site owners have access to your Facebook profile data, who sees it and what actions are turned into news stories and published on your Facebook Wall. In this way, it serves as a bridge between users' interaction with your Web site and their Facebook network.

To integrate Facebook Connect with your Web site, you must register and receive an API (Application Programming Interface) key via the Facebook Developer App page. An API is a set of common code standards that allow third-party developers to build software that can interoperate with the Facebook Platform. It is free to register for a Facebook API key and to implement Facebook Connect on your Web site.

Once you have your API key, you can create a new Facebook app and configure it to point to your Web address. This is done through the Callback URL field (see Figure 15-4).

You must already be a Facebook member to register for a Facebook Developer API key.

Registering for an API key

Following are the steps that you can take to register for an API key, if you are not already a Facebook app developer:

1. **Scroll to the bottom of your screen and click the Developers link.**

   You see the Facebook Developers page.

2. **Near the top of your screen, click the Start Now button.**

   The Get Started page appears.

3. **In the middle of your screen, click the Go to the Facebook Developer App link.**

   The Facebook Developer app begins the install process. You'll need to click Allow access the first time you click the link to get to the Developer page.

4. **At the top of the Developer page, click the Set Up New Application button.**

   The Create Application page appears.

5. **Type the name of your app.**

   Note: You must create an app within Facebook in order to receive an API key that allows you to integrate Facebook Connect on your Web site.

   To read the Facebook Terms of Agreement, you can click the link.

6. **Click Agree, and then click the Save Changes button.**

   Please note, if you disagree to the terms, you receive a Validation Failed alert and won't be able to proceed.

Congratulations, you are now officially a registered Facebook app developer and have a unique API key. In addition to developing Facebook apps, you can now integrate Facebook Connect within your Web site or iPhone app.

Setting up a new Facebook Connect app

After receiving your API key (or if you already are already a registered Facebook developer), click the Edit settings link from the My Application page. Here, you can edit your other app developer information (see Figure 15-4).

- **Essential Information:** You are assigned an application ID, an API key, and a secret code. Do not share your API key with anyone (except your trusted Web developer).

- **Basic Information:** You can type a description, upload an icon or logo, select your language, and add or remove developers to the project.

- **Contact Information:** You can enter the developer's contact e-mail, which is where Facebook can most easily contact you. There's also a field for user support e-mail, which is more of a customer support function.

- **User-facing URLs:** Here, you are asked to add links to display a help URL, a privacy URL, and a terms of service URL. You can link to your Web site pages or internally to your Facebook Page and user support e-mail (they can be the same person, or could route to two entirely different departments.)

Click Save to store your Application Settings information. You'll be taken to the My Applications page.

You can also choose to leave these fields blank, but it's always a good idea for a business Web site (or Facebook Page for that matter) to provide a Help page, a Privacy page, and a Terms of Service statement. It serves to protect the organization from a legal standpoint, and provides users with an upfront perspective of their rights.

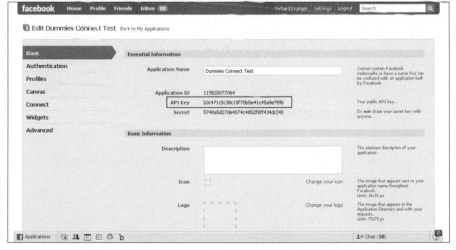

Figure 15-4:
Facebook provides developers with a unique API key.

Add a Fan Box to your Facebook Connected site and drive more Facebook fans. Just cut-and-paste a line of code. It's that simple.

Finding developer support and resources

Facebook provides comprehensive online support for their devoted developer community. On the Facebook Connect page, you find documentation to get started, as well as sample apps, source code, and iPhone support.

This material is intended for technical geeks; marketers need not read!

You can get to the Facebook Connect resources in three easy steps:

1. **Scroll to the bottom of your screen, and then click the Developers link.**

   The Facebook Developers page appears.

2. **At the top of your page, choose Resources⇨Facebook Connect.**

   The Facebook Connect page provides you with detailed information about Facebook Connect APIs and the way members can share content and actions with Facebook friends.

3. **Click the blue Connect With Facebook button to go to the Facebook Connect Developer Community/Resources page.**

Here, you'll find plenty of information to get you started in your Facebook Connect implementation. You'll also find links to discussion, view source, history, and Watch, which adds Facebook Connect to your watch list. You'll also find links to a more technical overview on the right side.

Facebook Developers info

A *wiki* (think Wikipedia, for example) is a collaborative Web site that is powered by a developer community. In Facebook's case, developers contribute in discussion forums, and add and edit a growing knowledge database that is easily searchable and accessible to all community members. (To view the main page of the Facebook Developer wiki, click the Documentation link at the top of any Facebook Developers page.)

For the technically astute, the tutorials, sample apps, script libraries, and best practices featured within the Facebook Developers pages should provide you with everything you need to integrate Facebook Connect with your Web site. And, for the rest of us, it's best to enlist the help of a knowledgeable Web developer who can offer recommendations on the best ways to engage users via Facebook Connect.

With the Facebook API, it's best for programmers to jump in and begin developing and testing new Facebook Connect implementations. This helps familiarize them with Facebook Platform and gives an idea of its possibilities and limitations. (See Figure 15-5.)

Finding Facebook Connect communities

From the Facebook Developer wiki page (click the Documentation link at the top of any Facebook Developers page), you can view a host of official and unofficial libraries and developer communities centered around developing apps for the Facebook Platform as well as implementing Facebook Connect. In the left column of the Facebook Developer wiki page, click the Client Libraries link. The company lists a number of developer libraries, along with links to both internal and external resources. The wiki also allows its community members to edit the list, keeping it fresh and up-to-date through people power.

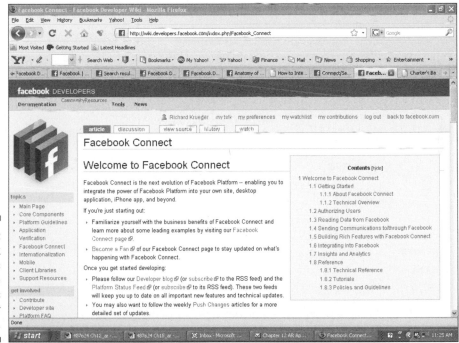

Figure 15-5: Facebook provides ample resources for developers.

Tracking bugs in Facebook apps and Facebook Connect

From the Client Libraries page, you can use the Bug Tracker for developers to document bugs and review related issues (even issues tracked by other developers) To register for a Bug Tracker account, at the top of any Facebook Developers page, choose Resources⇨Bug Tracker. The Facebook Platform bug tracking system displays (see Figure 15-6), where you can create an account, browse existing bug reports, enter a new bug or feature request, and view the most popular bugs. You'll find easy navigation within the Bug Tracker via tabs at the top of the Bug Tracker page that link to the Bug Main, New Bug, Search, Browse, and Help pages.

Facebook Connect news resources

Because Facebook is continuously adding new capabilities to its Facebook Platform API and Facebook Connect extension, it's a good idea to check the Facebook Developers News section often. You find the News tab on the top menu of any Facebook Developers page. Click the News tab to view the News page with the menu tabs Blog, Press (guidelines regarding partner press releases), and Platform Updates. The Platform Updates page provides a stream of developer-related updates. The brief news stories keep developers informed of changes, bug issues, and beta programs.

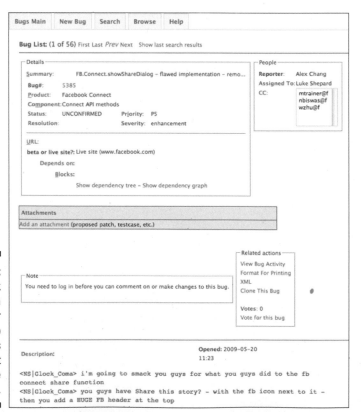

Figure 15-6:
Facebook
provides a
bug tracker
to help
developers
document
software
bugs.

Ben & Jerry's serves up a tasty Facebook Connect treat

Known as an environmentally-conscience purveyor of quality ice cream with a penchant for outrageous flavors, Vermont's own Ben & Jerry's has a loyal fan base that feel a powerful connection to the brand. The company wanted to translate that connection into social engagement via a compelling Facebook Connect implementation.

They decided to offer a social experience around their flavors (63 in all). Visitors who log in using Facebook Connect on the Ben & Jerry's Flavors page (go to www.benjerry.com and click the Flavors link on the top menu) can declare themselves a fan of a particular flavor, leave a comment, and post to their Facebook profile for all their friends to see. Another element of viral marketing is the ease in which you can invite up to eight of your Facebook friends.

While few companies attain a brand following enjoyed by Ben & Jerry's, we can all learn from respected marketers who take risks and stand on the leading edge of technology. Obviously, the company's strategy is working, as Ben & Jerry's has amassed over 930,000 fans to its Facebook Page. By the way, Rich's favorite flavor is Karamel Sutra and he's proud to be a fan.

Part V
The Part of Tens

The 5th Wave   By Rich Tennant

"I hope you're doing something online. A group like yours shouldn't be just playing street corners."

In this part . . .

These short chapters are packed with easy ideas and recommendations to help you convert others within your organization into Facebook believers.

We cover why your organization needs to be on Facebook, rules for customer engagement, and how best to conduct yourself on the social network. We give you places to go to stay up-to-date on the latest happenings, trends, and news regarding the Facebook Platform. And we suggest some applications that can truly enhance your business presence on Facebook.

Chapter 16

Ten Reasons Why Your Business Needs a Facebook Page

• •

*T*he Facebook Platform is no longer for young kids, college students, or young adults just keeping in touch with their best friends; it's turning into one of the most powerful platforms for business since Google launched AdWords in 2001.

Where else in reality — or on the Web — can you find some of the most connected and social people on the planet all ready and willing to engage with you and your business? Better still, where can you find an ad platform that can not only target by keyword (like Google can do) but also target by age, sex, location, and personal attributes such as favorite types of music, movies, or food? This chapter lists ten reasons to consider a Facebook Page for your business.

Get More Attention from Search Engines

One of the best things about a Page on Facebook is the ability for that Page to be indexed by the major search engines and appear in a search for your company name within days. Both profiles and Pages are indexed and considered a strong source of relevant content in the eyes of the search engines. Much like a blog where there are frequent posts of fresh content, so goes your Facebook presence. For businesses, this can be an invaluable way to drive more traffic to your Page.

Tap into the Social Network Community

Another benefit of having a Page for your business is that anyone can find your business on Facebook in ways perhaps that you never dreamed of. Sure, they can find your business by doing a search, but the real beauty of Facebook is the numerous ways that your business can be found just by being part of Facebook and updating your content regularly. Friends of fans can experience your business by seeing any updates you post from your Page to their friend's News Feed. Fans can share and pass along your Page to others, thereby helping you to tap into a new audience for your business with their endorsement!

Target a Global Digital Audience

The World Wide Web is global in nature and anyone can find your business on the Web if they know what to look for. While Facebook's membership keeps growing, you have an opportunity to get your business noticed by some of the most connected people on the Web today across the globe. Think about your ideal customer and the hobbies and activities they enjoy. If being on the Web and being social sounds like a fit for your audience, then Facebook is the place for your business. Moreover, as Facebook builds their audience on a global basis, you are right there for them.

Attract Unlimited New Clients

Unlike your profile where Facebook limits the number of friends you can have to 5,000, your Facebook Page can have an unlimited number of fans. This is why you want to update your Page regularly with interesting content. If you want to attract thousands to your Page, then consider the quality and the frequency by which you can post content. This is the key to building an unlimited number of fans.

Engage Your Audience

Facebook is free for everyone. So why wouldn't you want to have more traffic, more awareness, more fans, and more business as a result? Adding a provocative discussion topic to your Facebook Page and inviting all your fans to comment actually allows your target audience to do some marketing for you because they can spread the word to their friends, who may not yet be a fan of your Page. In doing so, they act as the viral accelerator to your marketing — free!

Sync Your Company Blog to Your Facebook Page

Although Facebook may be free, the need to create content to attract an audience is not. This challenge is not unique to Facebook; it affects all forms of social media and social networking. Being aware that you need a strong content creation engine is good, but be sure your content flows from one form of social media to your other forms of social media. In other words, if you have a company blog, be sure that you synchronize it with your Facebook Page so that when you post to your blog, the content posts to your Facebook Page for your Facebook audience to read.

Run a Promotion Just for Your Fans

When you have something to send to your entire fan base, you can do it with Facebook. This is a great way of re-engaging them with your business. If you want to run a promotion or send a discount to drive them to your offline store, you can do that. But don't forget to track your efforts; you can close the loop and have a way to track the effectiveness of this option. This could be as simple as collecting the coupon code you used, having a check box on an order form to gauge where the lead came from, or asking the caller if they are calling into your call center. You don't want to lose the opportunity to see how much business and return on investment you can have from this medium.

Facilitate Fan-to-Fan Interaction

Another important consideration when thinking about starting a Facebook Page is the ability to encourage fan-to-fan interaction. Where else can you get a platform that allows your best fans to talk with each other? This can be exceptionally helpful in some industries that have complex products. Your Page can work as an outpost where fans can support each other by answering questions and providing tips on how to make your product work better. Moreover, it works like a year-round focus group. Use your Wall to generate and actively try to keep the conversation going.

Host a Fabulous Event

Using Facebook Events is a great way of getting people together virtually or in person to support your local business, brand, or product. Events are also a very economical way of getting the word out beyond your normal in-house marketing list by inviting the fans of your Page (or members of your Group). Fans can also help you promote your Facebook Event to their friends by sharing the event if it seems of value to their friends.

Promote a Worthy Cause

Take a tip from Lance Armstrong, the world famous bicyclist, who is also known for his participation on social networks. His Facebook Page has 336,000 members. He brands himself relative to his expertise and what he's known for, being a bicyclist and the founder of LIVESTRONG. Armstrong provides up-to-date notices on his latest races, as well as videos and pictures of his current location and different bikes that he likes. More importantly, he uses his page to promote his LIVESTRONG cause. Social media is the perfect tool to unite fans around an issue that matters to you.

Chapter 17

Ten Business Etiquette Tips for Facebook

· ·

As Facebook grows so do the surprising number of faux pas committed by individuals and companies alike. The occasional slip of the tongue, the odd photo, and of course everyone's favorite: the embarrassing tag in a note or video.

You can and must protect your brand's reputation on Facebook, as well as maintain the utmost respect for the Facebook community. The downside is steep; you can lose your Page, your profile, or both. Once you are banned from Facebook, it's hard to get back in and by that time the audience that you worked so hard to build is gone. Therefore, it's a good idea to listen to the tips and warnings we outline in this chapter.

Don't Forget Birthday Greetings

With the power of Facebook, you can never forget a birthday of any of your friends. Then why not make it a point each day to see if fans of your Page are having a birthday? For sure, you should send them a birthday wish. You might even want to send them a virtual gift. And if that isn't enough, perhaps you want to offer them something unique that only you can provide for their birthday. For example, fans might be open to getting a happy birthday greeting from a local restaurant with an offer to come in that week for a free dessert or free drink.

The power of this platform is there — and surprisingly few Pages take advantage of this.

Don't Drink and Facebook

This should go without saying, but sometimes (at least) our ability to communicate is impaired by drinking. Drinking and e-mailing, twittering, and social networking just don't go together. You are better off not logging in. It only takes one bad or off color Wall post to get you reported in Facebook. Facebook members tend to be vigilant about things that they find offensive so just say no to drinking and Facebook.

Keep It Clean

Here is another no-no. Facebook does not allow users to send threatening, harassing, or sexually explicit messages to its members. Also, unsolicited messages are not tolerated. You should refrain from any of this behavior because the downside is your account could be warned, banned, and eventually disabled. What's worse, Facebook won't provide you with a description or copy of the content that was found to be offensive. Facebook does not provide any specifics on the limits that are enforced. Err on the side of caution if you think there is a question.

Avoid Overdoing It

You can over indulge in Facebook several ways, so you should watch out for these traps because they are very easy to fall into. First, don't randomly add people to your profile in the hopes of converting them to your Page. Befriending random people is considered poor form and may make you look like a stalker. Also, avoid over poking. Poking is an impersonal form of communication, so poking a friend can be fun but poking a stranger is poor form — so don't do it.

Dress Your Page Up with Applications

An endless sea of applications has been written for Facebook by independent developers. One or more of those could make a great fit for your business, so find an application or two (but no more) that you can use to make your Page more engaging. The nice thing is applications are easy to install and don't require any knowledge of how to build or modify them. Consider creating individual tabs for each application because each tab has a unique URL. You can even send out an e-mail to your customer base asking people to engage with your new application (for example, a survey application).

Respect the Wall

Your Wall is one of the most important places on your Page. It is where your fans can leave you messages and start a discussion on a topic. All messages on your Wall are visible to everyone who is a fan of your business or anyone who visits your Page. Think of it as a place of public record, so avoid editing comments on your Wall you don't like and always sound professional and courteous to anyone posting. Thank them for posting and make it fun for them and others.

Be Careful When Talking to Strangers

Sometimes written communication can seem flat and impersonal so choose your words carefully and be sure to re-read your responses, especially if the situation is or was getting heated. Better yet, if you think it is getting too heated, feel free to take it offline. Nothing beats the old-fashioned form of communication — the telephone — to help you get your point across and de-escalate a situation.

Don't Be Afraid to Ignore a Fan

Many people feel compelled to respond to every message in their e-mail Inbox. Similarly in Facebook people feel the need to respond to every comment or posting. Sometimes fans can overuse the various communication features in Facebook. New fans can sometimes binge on the information you present. Some good guidelines are: always welcome new fans, respond to comments and posts on your Wall in 24 hours but try to know when to respond and when to let the conversation rest. If a fan is irate, that's another thing; ignoring them can often work against you.

Deal with Your Irate Fans

Irate fans pose one of the biggest challenges this new medium has to offer. You have several ways to deal with an irate fan:

- ✔ Honestly consider their point and try to find something (anything) to agree with. Finding and establishing common ground is a great way to get the conversation back on track.

- ✔ Correct factual inaccuracies in a very tactful and pleasant way. The fan may not have all the data, which could be causing him to be irate.

- ✔ If you don't know the solution to a particular situation, don't bluff your way out of it — be sure to state that, commit to finding out more, and give them a date that you'll get back to them.

- ✔ Don't forget you can always take your conversation offline.

Maintain Your Privacy

For some business owners, privacy is a very important point. If you are a local business owner — say, the owner of a local jewelry store — you might not want to have your home address listed in the information section of your profile. Also, be sure the settings on your profile are set to Private (which is the default) rather than Public, which makes your personal information — including your home address — available to Internet search engines. Finally, be careful what groups you join. If someone you know in business is viewing your profile and sees controversial political, sexual, or religious activist groups on your profile, you may never find out why they stopped coming to your store.

Chapter 18

Ten Facebook Blogs for Business

Marketing on Facebook is truly unlike any other style of marketing. Now that you're well on your way to becoming a Facebook marketing master, you'll need to keep your knowledge of this ever-changing world up to date. There is no better way to get fast, up-to-date information than via the blogosphere.

Our goal is to give you some lasting tools for your continued education on Facebook. We monitored these blogs during the writing of this book to stay current on any possible changes coming from Facebook.

Facebook Blog

We wish we could say that one source is tops for news about Facebook, but in reality, we can't. However, the Facebook blog run by the Facebook employees is darn close. Here you can find out what's happening behind the scenes at Facebook. Facebook employees give firsthand accounts of new features, products, and goings-on around the office. Monitor this blog for changes to Facebook and interfacing directly with select Facebook employees. You can find this blog at http://blog.facebook.com.

AboutFaceDigital

Truth is, this is your authors' blog, where our goal is to find the latest Facebook news and echo it in one spot for marketers. At www.aboutfacedigital.com, we monitor numerous blogs and more for relevant Facebook news — even before we started writing the book. Now that we can focus on our own continued education, Rich's blog brings you case studies and examples of best practices along with the changes in the Facebook landscape. Also, check out Paul Dunay's blog called Buzz Marketing for Technology (www.buzzmarketingfortechnology.com) where he covers how to use social media specifically for tech firms of all sizes.

Inside Facebook

This independent blog (www.insidefacebook.com) focuses on Facebook and the Facebook Platform for developers and marketers. Inside Facebook began in April 2006 and delivers very timely information that tends to be quite technical in nature, which is why it appeals to the application developer community, as well as the more advanced social media marketer.

Facebook Advice

From the co-authors of the book *I'm on Facebook — Now What?* (Happy About, 2008), (www.facebookadvice.com) is co-run by Jason Alba and Jesse Stay. You can expect a wide range of topics, and not all are purely business oriented. You can count on them to keep you informed on trends for Facebook for business, Facebook for non profits, Facebook for education, and Facebook etiquette. Jason Alba also recently authored *I'm on LinkedIn — Now What???* (Happy About, 2009) and is the CEO and founder of JibberJobber (www.jibberjobber.com). Jesse is the founder of SocialOptimize and is an active Facebook developer, consultant, and expert.

Face Reviews

Rodney Rumford and his team at Gravitational Media LLC run Face Reviews (www.facereviews.com), another great source for Facebook applications reviews and Facebook news. They also cover the social media and social networks Twitter, MySpace, Bebo, FriendFeed, and OpenSocial to name a few.

We recommend their e-book *Twitter as a Business Tool* for anyone just getting started with Twitter — or even the seasoned Twitter professional. You never know when you can pick up a trick or two by reading something like this.

Why Facebook?

Run by Mari Smith, who is an independent consultant and coach. Her blog is great for social networking for both fun and profit. Mari addresses all things Facebook, as well as other popular social media tools like Twitter. The blog also offers the *7 Day Facebook Marketing Tips* by e-mail subscription. This could be very useful for those of you looking to keep on top of Facebook trends without having to go to your RSS feed reader. Also check out her quick start guide to social marketing, a fast track Webinar to help you accelerate your social media results. You can find her blog at www.whyfacebook.com.

Stayin' Alive

Jesse Stay, mentioned earlier in the chapter, also writes his own blog, consults with his business, Stay N' Alive Productions, LLC, and runs a social relationship management company called SocialToo.com. Jesse is one of the blogging pioneers in the social media space. His blog can be found at www.staynalive.com. Jesse provides valuable content, shares his knowledge on social media, technology, and new media, and posts the occasional rant.

Mashable

The quintessential guide to social media on the blogosphere, Mashable (www.mashable.com) covers much more than just Facebook. In fact, you can expect over five posts a day on Mashable to cover topics about Facebook, Twitter, MySpace, RSS, Flickr, FriendFeed, Seesmic, and much more. We highly recommend this blog for its diversity of authors and viewpoints as well as its diversity of topics pertaining to all things social media. They also do a lot of how-to guides and list great resources.

The Facebook Effect

The Facebook Effect is a blog that tracks Facebook news, commentary, and analysis. The Facebook Effect was founded in April 2007 to analyze the growing effects that Facebook has on the way we communicate, organize, share, and collaborate. They explore privacy issues, network effects of Facebook, trends and news, and provide those interested with information to help make sense of the increasingly important role Facebook plays in the lives of its millions of users around the world. The Facebook Effect has migrated completely to Facebook now and can only be accessed via its Facebook Page.

All Facebook

All Facebook (www.allfacebook.com) bills itself as the "unofficial" Facebook resource blog. We agree and look to this blog as *the* source of great information on Facebook demographics (they have a nice application resident on their site for this). They also have great stats on the top Facebook Pages, fastest growing pages, and least visited pages, plus plenty of data on Facebook Applications like the fastest growing, the best, the worst, and a ranking of the top Facebook application developers.

Chapter 19

Ten (Plus One) Must-Have Facebook Applications for Your Business

. . . .

*F*acebook offers a wide variety of applications (apps) geared to the business member. In fact, the Applications Directory lists more than 800 Facebook business apps at last glance (see Chapter 12). With so much free software just a click away, it's hard to know the must-have, timesaving, moneymaking, and productivity increasing apps that you may want for your Facebook business presence.

So, to help you narrow the selection and make sense of all these apps, we took some time to review many of the built-in Facebook apps and selected the following eleven apps (in no particular order) for your Page.

My Network Value (powered by XING)

Recognize your value within your network of contacts and tap into it to expand your net worth. My Network Value helps you evaluate your value and then compare it to others in your network. From social networking pioneer Xing, this application lets you discover new business contacts and opportunities through searches and advanced contact management tools. (See Figure 19-1.)

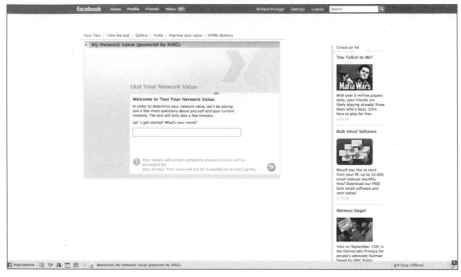

Figure 19-1:
Find out your value within your network with Xing's My Network Value.

MyOffice

Ideal for team members spread across different office locations, MyOffice helps you to manage your project or business with a collaborative suite of tools. Schedule meetings with your team or group, organize an event, discuss ideas, share files, create to-do lists, collaborate on docs and whiteboards, and assign tasks to increase productivity. MyOffice lets you quickly and easily collaborate with your colleagues, partners, or clients.

Tag Biz Pro Business Cards

Business card apps are fairly common on Facebook these days. But Tag Biz Pro stands out from the pack with a realistic index card design and a bunch of networking features built in. The app allows you to do the following:

✔ Create a business card and customize it

✔ Attach your business card to Facebook messages

✔ Browse other cards and read comments

✔ Let others know what you are looking for

Anyone who is interested in doing business on Facebook should use Tag Biz Pro. The Tag Biz Pro automates the relationship networking and referral process by creating a tag cloud, or cluster of words describing your business. Pick your keywords, invite your friends, and build your own business network with this professional networking app. (See Figure 19-2.)

Figure 19-2:
Create your own virtual business card with Tag Biz Pro.

Linkedin Answers

Social networks don't have to be separate islands. From the folks at the popular professional networking site Linkedin comes Linkedin Answers, which allows you to tap into the wisdom of the Linkedin community by posting questions that anyone can answer. Likewise, you can also answer questions if the subject is within your expertise, which is a great way to build your brand's credibility. (See Figure 19-3.)

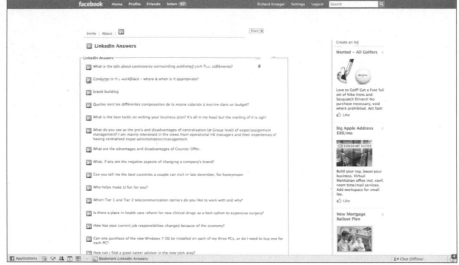

Figure 19-3:
Tap into the
wisdom
of the
crowd with
LinkedIn
Answers.

SlideShare

The Web's largest community for sharing presentations makes it easy to
post your presentations to your Facebook Page. With SlideShare, you can
upload your PowerPoint, PDF, Word, and Keynote presentations so that others
in your network can view them. You can even embed YouTube videos in your
presentations and add audio to make professional looking Webinars. (See
Figure 19-4.)

Figure 19-4:
Post your
own or
choose from
SlideShare's
extensive
library of
presen-
tations.

Static FBML

Although Facebook Pages are limited in terms of design customization, you can add the Static FBML app to any Page to integrate HTML directly on the Page. Developed internally by Facebook developers, this app lets you enter HTML or FBML (Facebook Markup Language) within a box for enhanced Page customization and added functionality. (See Figure 19-5.)

Figure 19-5:
If you want to add some HTML to your Facebook Page, Static FBML is the app for you.

FlashPlay

If you're looking to add more flash to your Page — and by that, we mean Flash movies, animations, scripts, and so on — FlashPlay allows you to add any Flash file to your Page and make it visible to everyone. Flash is an Internet standard that supports videos, such as those found on YouTube, as well as games. You may also browse the FlashPlay library to find a selection of popular games, animations, and apps that can make your Page stand out. (See Figure 19-6.)

Figure 19-6:
Let your
Page stand
out with
a little
Flash from
FlashPlay.

what.io

Another great app not yet available for Pages, what.io allows you to quickly save your IOUs. When installed, the IOUs are displayed as post-it notes on your profile. You can print IOU certificates and share with friends, and don't forget that $50 you loaned your buddy on your last road trip to Vegas! The service works easily with friends who are not yet on Facebook via their e-mail address.

PRX Builder

Based on the original Social Media Press Release (SMPR) Template from Todd Defren of SHIFT Communications, PRX Builder helps you easily create the next generation of press releases. Enhance your press release with new media elements, such as links, multimedia, and social media service buttons for digg and del.icio.us. Automatically add Technorati tags and then distribute your release through PR Newswire. The service also optimizes your releases for higher visibility within Technorati and Google Blog Search. You can even moderate any comments your SMPR may receive. RSS and e-mail subscription options make this an invaluable tool for companies looking to get the word out. And the best part is the service is free! (See Figure 19-7.)

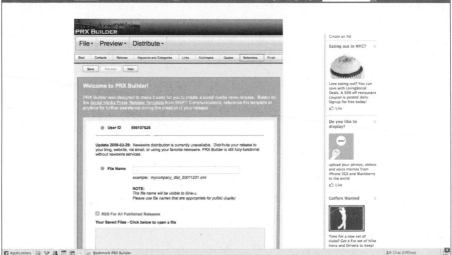

Figure 19-7:
Create
a social
media press
release to
promote
your busi-
ness with
PRX Builder.

Page Maps

Ideal for companies with a physical presence, Page Maps allows you to add a custom map to your Page or personal profile. You can show your business locations or favorite spots around town. It displays a mini map requiring no additional clicks to see, and links to a larger map or directions. (See Figure 19-8.)

Figure 19-8:
Create a
map
pinpointing
where your
business is
located.

Phonebook

How many times has one of your co-workers asked you for a contact? Phonebook let's you share your Rolodex in a secure environment. You can also attach e-mails and notes to contacts, back up your list, and exchange and compare contacts with your associates. Maybe now your staff won't call you at 9 o'clock in the morning the next time they can't find a number and you're away on vacation!

Appendix A

Web Links for Facebook Marketing

*F*acebook offers you the opportunity to build new and develop existing business relationships. A completely self-contained universe, Facebook has plenty of tools that can help you to find and then connect with your target audience. From setting up your business presence on a Facebook Page to advertising to a highly-targeted consumer base to providing a Marketplace where you can buy and sell your goods and services, the following links can provide you with some basic building blocks to help you further develop your Facebook strategy.

Facebook Pages Directory

A searchable directory of all Facebook Pages, this organizes Pages according to which ones have the most fans. You can also view more links according to vertical Page directories, including: places, products, services, stores, restaurants, bars and clubs, organizations, politicians, government officials, non-profits, TV shows, films, games, sports teams, celebrities/public figures, music, and Web sites.

www.facebook.com/pages

Facebook Marketing Solutions Page

Want to see what's working for other Facebook marketers? The Facebook Marketing Solutions page is the place to go where you can also contribute to the conversation (see Figure A-1).

www.facebook.com/marketing

Facebook Lexicon Tool

The Facebook Lexicon application keeps on getting better for marketers interested in knowing what people are saying. Type a term and see how much buzz it's garnering within Facebook.

www.facebook.com/lexicon

Facebook Friend Finder

With this handy friend finder page, Facebook offers a number of ways to search for your friends. You can type a name or an e-mail address, or search by a school or an employer.

www.facebook.com/find-friends

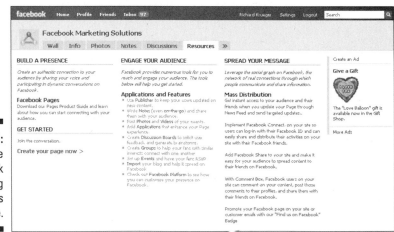

Figure A-1:
The Facebook Marketing Solutions page.

Facebook Help

Confused about a Facebook feature or function? Facebook provides a searchable Help database that explains terms in easy-to-understand language (see Figure A-2).

www.facebook.com/help.php

Facebook Advertising

The Facebook self-serve advertising system is easily accessible from a link at the bottom of any Facebook page. It lets you create your own ads, target your audience, and set a budget to optimize your returns.

www.facebook.com/advertising

Facebook Developer Resources

For developers interested in building applications for the Facebook platform, Facebook offers ample documentation and resources. Here you'll find tools, script libraries, and forums to help you develop compelling applications.

http://developers.facebook.com

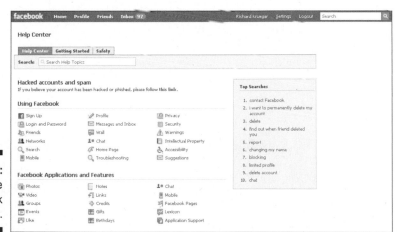

Figure A-2: The Facebook Help Center.

Facebook Marketing Primer

This presentation walks you through the many marketing opportunities available in Facebook. From building a company presence with a free Facebook Page to launching an advertising campaign on the self-serve advertising platform to selling products via its Marketplace, this primer is a straight-forward overview on how to market your business in the world's largest social network.

www.slideshare.net/rkrueger/krueger-facebook-marketing

Five Tips for Improving Your Landing Tab

From the popular Facebook blog AllFaceBook.com, Facebook advertisers can benefit from this helpful guide. As you tap into the micro-targeting advertising platform, you will want to use tabs to create an effective landing page for your Facebook audience.

www.allfacebook.com/2009/08/how-to-create-a-landing-tab-
that-converts-new-visitors-into-fans/

Five Tips for Optimizing Your Facebook Page

Like a Web site, a Facebook presence is a fundamental tactic for all social network marketers, and should be on everyone's list of must haves. But once you build it, you'll need a strategy for posting updates as frequently as you can with interesting content.

www.buzzmarketingfortech.blogspot.com/2009/06/5-tips-for-
optimizing-your-facebook.html

Five Ways Facebook Will Get You Fired

More than half of all employers monitor your computer activities. Find out the most important ways to protect your online reputation and keep your job in this helpful eBook.

www.aboutfacedigital.com/blog/2009/08/18/facebook-can-get-
you-fired/

Facebook Applications Tracking

Facebook developers and marketers alike can now pay close attention to which applications are catching on, thanks to Adonomics. This Web site charts the top performing Facebook applications across several categories (see Figure A-3).

www.adonomics.com

Figure A-3:
Track
Facebook
applica-
tions and
see how
they rank
per number
of monthly
users.

The Adonomics 100™

Rank	Company	Daily Active Users	Valuation
1	Zynga	4,675,441	$121,986,913
2	Playfish Ltd	4,218,008	$53,653,919
3	Rock You	2,140,355	$63,067,230
4	Slide	1,681,919	$55,793,168
5	Facebook	958,105	$7,638,216
6	Flixster	955,084	$22,004,638
7	Project Agape	944,178	$31,943,509
8	FamilyLink.com	771,873	$9,562,005
9	SA Ventures	677,760	$7,698,577
10	SNAP Interactive	626,980	$11,103,130
11	Watercooler, Inc.	489,308	$10,965,984
12	Zoosk	453,853	$2,354,335
13	MindJolt.com	391,857	$1,674,730
14	iLike	361,736	$6,319,667
15	SC Ventures	351,768	$2,994,517
16	Chainn Inc.	316,056	$6,345,549
17	Big Dates	241,473	$2,536,202
18	Social Gaming Network (SGN)	226,280	$6,077,927
19	Dan Peguine	188,007	$1,449,718
20	TS Ventures	148,231	$1,437,875

Samepoint Social Media Search

Find out what people are saying about a company, a product, or even you. Samepoint searches the social Web, including Facebook, Twitter, Digg, YouTube, and many more, to bring back relevant results about social net-work conversations.You can even search by social media type (that is, just video sites) and create RSS Feeds that continuously update the information on your Page as new content is found (see Figure A-4).

www.samepoint.com

How Sociable Are You

Measure your brand's visibility across 22 metrics based on the most popular social media sites with this free and easy to-use tool.

www.howsociable.com

Figure A-4: Search for conversations across the social Web using Samepoint. com.

Addict-o-matic

A social media search engine, Addict-o-matic offers a nice, real-time view into what people are saying about a particular search term (see Figure A-5).

www.addictomatic.com

Technorati Blog Search

Offering the most comprehensive directory of blogs on the Web, Technorati helps you to identify all the top blogs within a given topic. You can also search all blogs indexed by Technorati, which is about 80 million on last count.

www.technorati.com

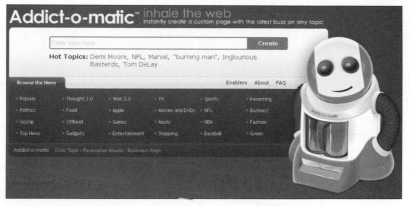

Figure A-5:
Create a
Facebook
Page with
real-time
news from
across the
social Web
with Addict-
o-matic.

Google Blog Search

Where would you find the best tool for searching blogs on the Web? Why Google, of course! Google's Blog Search offers advanced search options where you can search by date, which is a handy feature for tracking word-of-mouth buzz.

    http://blogsearch.google.com

BlogPulse

An easy-to-use, free tool, BlogPulse lets you type up to five search terms and then get a visual representation of how much buzz each term garners, which is measured in terms of social media mentions. Excellent for competitive analysis, BlogPulse buzz graphs can help a marketer to quantify their social media campaigns (see Figure A-6).

    www.blogpulse.com

Google Trends Lab

Another helpful tool from Google is the Google Trends lab, which shows you how many searches and news stories a given search term has generated.

    http://trends.google.com

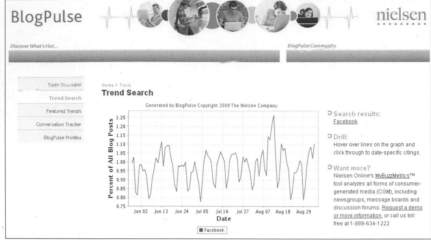

Figure A-6:
BlogPulse,
from TV
ratings
company
Nielsen,
charts
keyword
use across
blogs.

BoardTracker

Bulletin boards, an open forum where users can post their opinions on a given topic, are still extremely popular on the social Web. You should pay attention to what's being said about you and your competitors across bulletin boards. This helpful search site brings most of these comments under one simple search interface.

www.boardtracker.com

Search Twitter

Twitter is an increasingly important source for all kinds of discussions. Twitter's own internal search engine lets you hone in on any tweets (that is, Twitter messages) that you should know about, and even allows you to create an RSS Feed for that search term, so that anytime the term appears in a tweet, you'll know about it.

http://search.twitter.com

Compete Web Traffic Analysis

The Compete site traffic analyzer is another helpful tool for evaluating how you're doing against your competition. Enter your Web site URL, and up to five other URLs, and watch as Compete creates a useful graph showing traffic to your site(s) based on monthly page views, site vistors, and several other metrics.

www.compete.com

Bit.ly URL Shortener

Given the limited space social network sites allow for you to enter content updates (such as, Facebook and Twitter), people looking to push out links are wise to use a URL shortener, such as the one from Bit.ly. Free and easy-to-use, Bit.ly creates an abbreviated URL out of your long links and even lets you track how much traffic you generated via the shortened link (see Figure A-7).

www.bit.ly

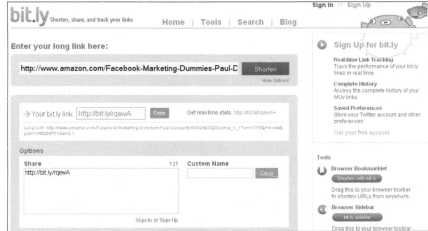

Figure A-7:
Shorten the
links on your
Facebook
Page using
this Web
site.

Digg Makes News Social

Primarily for news, links, images, and videos, Digg lets you submit news stories, and then vote on the importance of those stories relative to all others.

www.digg.com

Truveo Aggregates Videos

Online videos continue to proliferate user-generated sites. Truveo lets you search across the major video sites, including YouTube and MotionBox, saving you time so that you don't have to visit those sites.

www.truveo.com

Appendix B

Protecting Your Identity in Facebook

*F*acebook doesn't provide a whole lot of privacy for your Page (see Chapter 4) since a Page is available on the Internet for all to see. You can't restrict access to your Page in external search engine results, such as Google, so you can't limit access to just employees, customers, or even Facebook members.

But, because reputations are made on Facebook, it helps to understand what you can control so that you can make more informed choices when sharing information with other Facebook members. Following are ten crucial privacy options for your personal profile that can help protect your professional reputation, your friends, and photos and videos of you.

Setting Privacy Controls

When it comes to privacy settings on Facebook, it's all about protecting information contained in your profile. Keep in mind that all business is also personal on Facebook, so review your personal privacy settings to help you balance out your professional and personal personas on the social network.

Hiding your contact info

When I realized that my friends had access to my contact information, it didn't immediately bother me. But, when my friends List grew to encompass much more than actual friends, I realized that it wasn't in my best interest to make my contact Information available to all of them.

Facebook lets you set privacy controls for your contact information. Following are steps to limit access to your contact information:

1. **Choose Settings⇨Privacy Settings on the top right navigation bar.**

2. **Click the Contact Information tab on the top of the page.**

   As shown in Figure B-1, you can adjust privacy settings for each field that makes up your contact information.

3. **Choose each field's privacy setting from each drop-down menu.**

   Fields include your IM screen name, mobile phone number, other phone number, current address, Web site, and e-mail address.

4. **Click Save Changes at the bottom of the page.**

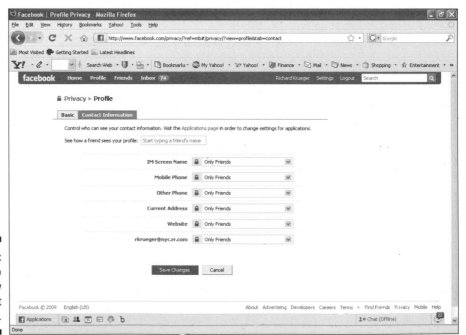

Figure B-1:
Limit who
can view
your contact
information.

Hiding your relationship status

Not everyone needs to know if you are married, single, or whether "it's complicated." Relationship status has caused many a break-up, at least one death in the UK from a jealous separated husband, and has probably affected the way your co-workers view you. To eliminate stories relating to your relationship status, follow these steps:

1. **Choose Settings⇨Privacy Settings on the top right navigation bar.**

2. **Select News Feed and Wall.**

3. **Click the Activities tab.**

4. **Uncheck the box next to Change Relationship Status.**

   This prevents stories regarding your relationship from being generated and distributed.

5. **Click Save Changes.**

Restricting photo/video tagging

Photos that you didn't even post could come back to haunt you thanks to the Facebook tagging feature (see Chapter 6). If you aren't careful with your privacy settings, photos and videos shot by someone else could be tagged or made public, causing serious ramifications to your career, social life, and general reputation.

Fortunately, Facebook provides settings that limit who can see photos (and videos) in which you're tagged. Following are the steps to limit distribution of tagged photos of you:

1. **Choose Settings⇨Privacy Settings on the top right navigation bar.**

2. **Click the Profile link.**

   Half-way down the page, you can view the Photos Tagged of You and Videos Tagged of You settings.

3. **Choose Customize from the Photos Tagged of You drop-down menu.**

   Even though these photos could reside on another member's profile, you can still limit who gets to see the photo.

4. Choose one of the following options:

- Everyone: Allows everyone to see tagged photos of you.

- Friends of Friends: Allows friends of your friends to view the tagged photos of you.

- Only Friends: Restricts the view to only your direct friends.

You can also exclude specific people by entering a friend's name or a friend List under *Block List*. Notice that when you enter either a friend's name or group name, Facebook presents you with names that match.

5. Click Okay at the bottom of the screen (see Figure B-2).

Figure B-2:
Limit who can view photos in which you are tagged.

Restricting News Feed stories

News Feed stories are generated whenever you interact with your Facebook Page (see Chapter 6), such as posting a new photo album, commenting on a note, adding a friend, or changing your relationship status. You might have professional reasons to limit who receives this News Feed information about you.

So don't be caught off-guard by News Feed stories being generated by your actions within Facebook. The News Feed and Wall Privacy settings allow you to opt-out of stories for these actions. Following are the steps to limit access to your News Feed stories:

1. **Choose Settings⇨Privacy Settings on the top right navigation bar.**

2. **Click the News Feed and Wall link.**

   Uncheck boxes on your Privacy — News Feed & Wall page (shown in Figure B-3) to restrict certain types of stories from being generated and distributed, including Wall posts, comments, profile information, discussions, new friends, and chats.

3. **Click Save Changes**.

Opting out of Facebook searches

Within the Facebook community, if you don't want to be found when someone searches for your name, college, or previous employer, then you can stop your personal profile from appearing in Facebook Search results. Note that by default your profile is available to people within your network.

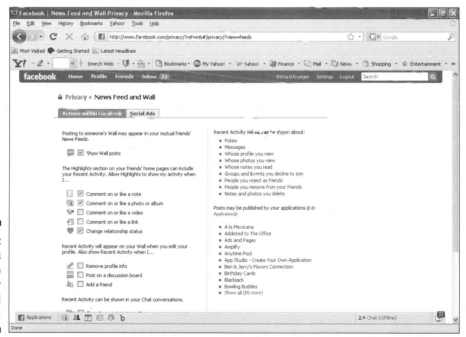

Figure B-3: Limit access to who views your News Feed stories.

To opt-out of internal Facebook searches, follow these simple steps:

1. **Choose Settings⇨Privacy Settings on the top right navigation bar.**

2. **In the Search Visibility drop-down menu (see Figure B-4), choose Only Friends.**

   Only friends who are confirmed friends of yours can see your profile in a Facebook Search.

3. **Click Save Changes.**

   By choosing Customize from the Search Visibility drop-down menu, you can refine your settings even more.

Protecting your friends List

One of the great things about Facebook is that you can see friends of your friends. This is an effective way to find new friends. However, some of your friends may not appreciate that they can be readily found from your friends List and you may not appreciate your friends befriending other friends of yours.

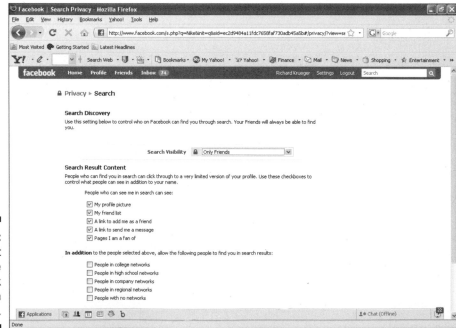

Figure B-4:
Opt-out of the Facebook Search feature.

So, Facebook lets you restrict who can see your friends. To change privacy settings for friends, follow these steps:

1. **Choose Settings⇨Privacy Settings on the top right navigation bar.**

2. **Click Profile.**

3. **Click the drop-down menu next to Friends, which is located about halfway down the page.**

4. **Select who can see your friends List.**

5. **Click Save Changes at the bottom of the page.**

   Your new privacy settings for who has access to your friends List are stored.

Evading external searches

Although search engines provide plenty of visibility for people who want to be found, they also present a problem for those who prefer to remain private. It surprises a lot of people that select information from your Facebook profile may appear in search engines. Although your entire profile is not exposed, your profile picture, list of friends, links to add you as a friend or send you a message, and a list of up to 20 Pages of which you are a fan is visible, by default, in Google and other external search engines.

Whatever your reason for not wanting your Facebook profile to be found via Google, follow these steps:

1. **Choose Settings⇨Privacy Settings on the top right navigation bar.**

2. **Click Search.**

3. **Uncheck the box next to Create a public search listing for me and submit it for search engine indexing. (See Figure B-5.)**

   Uncheck this box to prevent search engines from indexing your Facebook profile.

4. **Click the Save Changes button.**

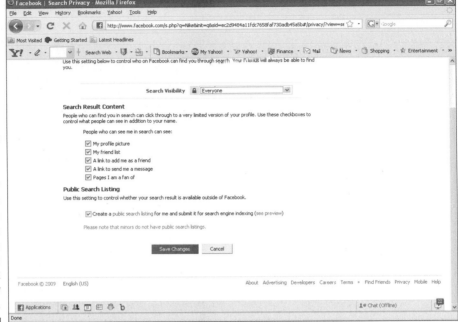

Figure B-5:
Protecting
your
personal
profile from
search
engine
results with
Facebook
Privacy
settings.

Restricting Application News Feed Stories

This one is part confessional. One of your authors had a slight obsession with a particular Bowling Buddies application by PlayFish. Let's face it, some of these casual gaming apps on Facebook can be downright addictive, and for him, this was his Tetris.

However, what he didn't realize was that every time he played a game, which was fairly often for a period, a news story would be published on his friend's profiles of his bowling prowess. After receiving comments from friends and work associates on how frequently he was playing Bowling Buddies, he realized that his actions were being broadcast to his friends via News Feed stories. Good thing he didn't install the What Sex and the City Charter Are You? app!

To restrict stories from being published on your interactions with Facebook applications (apps), follow these steps:

1 Choose Settings⇨Application Settings on the top right navigation bar.

Facebook displays a list of your recently used apps, as shown in Figure B-6.

Figure B-6:
Choose to
opt-out of
application-
related
stories.

2. **Click the Settings tab.**

3. **Select each application that you want to share.**

You can also choose Customize to exclude certain friends from seeing
these stories.

4. **Click OK.**

Setting Up a Friends List

If you want to share a specific photo album, video, or post with a subset of
your friends, friends Lists are for you (see Figure B-7). You can organize your
friends into groups, such as co-workers, family, or classmates. And then you
can identify which groups has access to specific content that you share.
For example, if you have pictures from your days as a college frat boy and
prefer that your co-workers not have access to those photos, you can restrict
access to just your college friends List when you post your updates.

Figure B-7:
A friends List lets you control who can see your content.

Setting Photo Album Controls

If you don't want your photos available to the world, not just those in which you're tagged, you need to configure the visibility of each photo album. After you've uploaded an album, you can specify who has access to those pictures.

1. **From your personal profile page, click the Photos tab.**

2. **Choose Create a Photo Album.**

   Next to Security, you see a drop-down menu labeled Who Can See This.

3. **Choose between My Networks and Friends, Friends of Friends, Only Friends, and Customize.**

   By selecting Customize, you can select which friends to exclude from seeing your album.

You can also change the privacy setting on all of your albums via your Settings menu on the top right of the page.

1. **Choose Settings⇨Privacy Settings on the top right navigation bar.**

2. **Beneath Photos Tagged of You, click the Edit Photo Albums Privacy Settings link.**

   This takes you to your Privacy — Photos page.

3. **Select the appropriate privacy option for each of your albums (see Figure B-8).**

4. **Click Save Changes.**

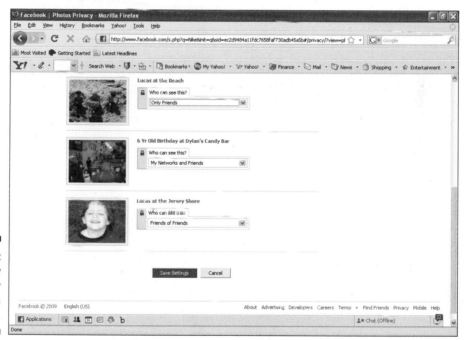

Figure B-8: Set privacy settings for each photo album.

Index

Business/Accounting & Bookkeeping
Bookkeeping For Dummies
978-0-7645-9848-7

eBay Business
All-in-One For Dummies,
2nd Edition
978-0-470-38536-4

Job Interviews
For Dummies,
3rd Edition
978-0-470-17748-8

Resumes For Dummies,
5th Edition
978-0-470-08037-5

Stock Investing
For Dummies,
3rd Edition
978-0-470-40114-9

Successful Time
Management
For Dummies
978-0-470-29034-7

Computer Hardware
BlackBerry For Dummies,
3rd Edition
978-0-470-45762-7

Computers For Seniors
For Dummies
978-0-470-24055-7

iPhone For Dummies,
2nd Edition
978-0-470-42342-4

Laptops For Dummies,
3rd Edition
978-0-470-27759-1

Macs For Dummies,
10th Edition
978-0-470-27817-8

Cooking & Entertaining
Cooking Basics
For Dummies,
3rd Edition
978-0-7645-7206-7

Wine For Dummies,
4th Edition
978-0-470-04579-4

Diet & Nutrition
Dieting For Dummies,
2nd Edition
978-0-7645-4149-0

Nutrition For Dummies,
4th Edition
978-0-471-79868-2

Weight Training
For Dummies,
3rd Edition
978-0-471-76845-6

Digital Photography
Digital Photography
For Dummies,
6th Edition
978-0-470-25074-7

Photoshop Elements 7
For Dummies
978-0-470-39700-8

Gardening
Gardening Basics
For Dummies
978-0-470-03749-2

Organic Gardening
For Dummies,
2nd Edition
978-0-470-43067-5

Green/Sustainable
Green Building
& Remodeling
For Dummies
978-0-470-17559-0

Green Cleaning
For Dummies
978-0-470-39106-8

Green IT For Dummies
978-0-470-38688-0

Health
Diabetes For Dummies,
3rd Edition
978-0-470-27086-8

Food Allergies
For Dummies
978-0-470-09584-3

Living Gluten-Free
For Dummies
978-0-471-77383-2

Hobbies/General
Chess For Dummies,
2nd Edition
978-0-7645-8404-6

Drawing For Dummies
978-0-7645-5476-6

Knitting For Dummies,
2nd Edition
978-0-470-28747-7

Organizing For Dummies
978-0-7645-5300-4

SuDoku For Dummies
978-0-470-01892-7

Home Improvement
Energy Efficient Homes
For Dummies
978-0-470-37602-7

Home Theater
For Dummies,
3rd Edition
978-0-470-41189-6

Living the Country Lifestyle
All-in-One For Dummies
978-0-470-43061-3

Solar Power Your Home
For Dummies
978-0-470-17569-9

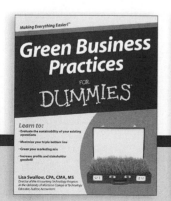

Available wherever books are sold. For more information or to order direct: U.S. customers visit www.dummies.com or call 1-877-762-2974.
U.K. customers visit www.wileyeurope.com or call (0) 1243 843291. Canadian customers visit www.wiley.ca or call 1-800-567-4797.

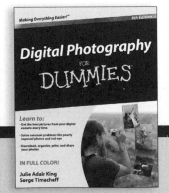